Pop Culture Pulse

The Beat of Modern Influencers

By
Peyton Gray

Pop
Culture Pulse

The Beat of Modern Influencers

Table of Contents

Introduction

Imagine waking up to the latest viral dance craze on TikTok or scrolling through Instagram to see what your favorite influencer is wearing today. If you've ever found yourself captivated by the online lives of social media stars and pop culture icons, you're not alone. Influencers have become an integral part of our daily existence, shaping our tastes, habits, and even our values. In a world where online presence can make or break a career, it's more important than ever to understand how this ecosystem works. You're about to dive deep into the fascinating realm where pop culture and digital influence intersect, changing the landscape of our society.

Over the past decade, the digital revolution has transformed the way we engage with popular culture. Gone are the days when celebrities were untouchable figures seen only in movies or on TV. Today, influencers offer a new level of accessibility, allowing fans to interact in real-time and even shape the content they produce. It's more than just entertainment; it's a social revolution that has redefined what it means to be influential. This shift has prompted teens like you to question, "What does it take to become an influencer?" or "How do these online personas impact my life?"

To understand this profound change, we first need to explore what makes influencers so compelling. They offer a blend of authenticity and intimacy that's hard to find elsewhere. With just a smartphone, they invite you into their lives, sharing everything from their morning routines to their deepest thoughts. This sense of connection makes you feel like you're part of their world, and that's incredibly powerful. As a result, influencers wield a level of influence that can rival, or even surpass, traditional celebrities. But how did we get here?

The rise of social media platforms like Instagram, YouTube, and TikTok has democratized fame. More than ever, everyday people can achieve superstar status, provided they have the right mix of talent, charisma, and strategy. Many influencers initially started as regular users, sharing their passions and talents. However, with the help of algorithms and viral trends, some of these users have amassed millions of followers. These platforms have redefined what it means to be successful and influential in the digital age. Yet, the allure of online fame comes with its own set of challenges and responsibilities.

So, what does it take to navigate this landscape successfully? To some, it might look easy—just post a few videos or snapshots, and fame will follow. However, the reality is far more complex. Building and maintaining an online presence requires relentless effort, meticulous planning, and a deep understanding of social media algorithms. Influencers constantly adapt to changing trends, all while staying authentic to their audience. It's a delicate balance that requires both creativity and business acumen.

As we journey through the intricacies of pop culture and digital influence, you'll see that there's much more happening behind the scenes. From monetization strategies to brand collaborations, influencers have turned their channels into lucrative careers. They have become marketing powerhouses, endorsing products and shaping consumer behaviors with just a single post. Yet, this commercial aspect brings its own set of ethical questions. How do influencers balance authenticity with sponsorships? Can they remain true to themselves while promoting brands?

Another essential aspect we'll explore is the role of diversity and representation in this new digital landscape. Influencers from various backgrounds now have a platform to share their stories and perspectives. This inclusivity is redefining societal norms and expectations, offering a broader range of role models for teens like you. However, it's not all glitter and glam. The pressure to maintain a public persona can take a toll on mental health. Many influencers face challenges like burnout and social scrutiny, making it crucial to address these issues openly and constructively.

Beyond the glamor and challenges, there's also a growing trend of influencers using their platforms for activism and social change. Digital movements have gained momentum, with influencers playing pivotal roles in raising awareness about social issues. Whether it's advocating for environmental causes or fighting for equality, social media has become a powerful tool for change. The future of influencing looks promising, with emerging trends pointing to even more profound impacts on our society. But what will this future look like, and how will it continue to shape our world?

This book is your guide to navigating this ever-evolving landscape. It will equip you with the knowledge to understand the mechanics of online fame, the economics of influence, and the social responsibilities that come with it. You'll learn about the dynamics of different social media platforms, the strategies behind viral content, and the real-world impact of digital activism. Each chapter will delve into these topics, providing a comprehensive understanding of how pop culture and influencers are transforming our everyday lives.

As you read through these pages, let curiosity be your guide. Question the content you consume, and think critically about the influences shaping your world. The goal is not just to inform, but to inspire you to become an active participant in this digital age. Whether you're dreaming of becoming the next big influencer or simply trying to understand the world around you, this book offers valuable insights to help you navigate this complex and fascinating landscape.

So, get ready to explore the captivating world of pop culture and digital influence. There's so much to discover, and it all starts here. Welcome to the journey.

Chapter 1:
The Rise of Pop Culture Influencers

The world has seen an incredible transformation in how influence is wielded, thanks to the digital age. Pop culture influencers are the driving force behind this shift, shaping trends and altering our daily lives in subtle yet profound ways. From beauty gurus to gaming enthusiasts, influencers have turned personal passions into global phenomena, creating communities that transcend geography. This chapter delves into the rise of these modern icons, exploring how they evolved from mere social media users to powerhouses of cultural influence. As we journey through this landscape, we'll uncover the dynamic interplay between technology and human connection, illustrating how influencers have redefined what it means to be influential in the 21st century.

Evolution of Influence

Pop culture influencers didn't just appear out of nowhere; their rise is part of a much larger story about how influence itself has evolved over time. Once upon a time, influence was almost exclusively the domain of celebrities, politicians, and business moguls. These individuals had the power to shape public opinion and trends because they controlled substantial resources or had access to powerful institutions. However, the advent of the internet and, more recently, social media has significantly democratized influence.

In the early days of the internet, forums and chat rooms were some of the first spaces where people could freely express their opinions and gather influence. These platforms allowed like-minded individuals to connect and build communities. Despite their rudimentary technology, they played a crucial role in shifting influence from traditional gatekeepers to everyday people. Someone who was knowledgeable about a specific topic could become a respected voice in that community.

As we moved into the 2000s, blogging emerged as a new form of influence. Bloggers were unique in that they didn't need a publishing house or a broadcasting network to reach an audience. Instead, they built their followings by producing consistent, high-quality content. From fashion to tech, bloggers set trends and provided in-depth insights that mainstream media couldn't always offer. Their influence was particularly notable because it represented a shift towards a more personalized and authentic form of content.

Social media platforms like MySpace and later Facebook, YouTube, and Twitter further accelerated this trend. Suddenly, anyone with an internet connection could potentially reach millions of people. The barriers to entry were incredibly low, and the algorithms favored content that resonated with large numbers of users. This created fertile ground for the rise of social media stars, who could build massive followings by curating relatable and engaging content.

YouTube, launched in 2005, was a game-changer. It wasn't just another social network; it was a broadcast platform available to everyone. Video content allowed a new kind of intimacy and authenticity, helping creators form deeper connections with their audiences. Early YouTube stars like Jenna Marbles and PewDiePie didn't start with high production values, but their genuine and often unpolished content resonated deeply with viewers.

Instagram's arrival added another layer to this evolution. While YouTube was perfect for longer, more in-depth content, Instagram's focus on photos and short videos made it ideal for quick, digestible updates. The platform's visual nature meant that aesthetics became paramount. This gave rise to a new kind of influencer: one who could create a visually captivating and curated feed. Filters, hashtags, and the ability to tag brands quickly turned Instagram into a marketing powerhouse.

With the proliferation of these platforms, we're no longer passive consumers of media. The feedback loop is stronger than ever; our likes, comments, and shares directly influence what gets shown to us and what trends emerge. This dynamic relationship between influencers and their audiences has shifted the balance of power. Influencers are more attuned to the immediate reactions of their audience, allowing them to adapt and stay relevant in real-time.

Influence today is multifaceted. It no longer requires a celebrity endorsement to make something popular. Micro and nano-influencers—those with smaller, niche followings—often command strong loyalty and trust, making them incredibly valuable, especially in specific markets. Their authenticity and relatability can be more compelling than the polished facade of traditional celebrities.

If we look at how brands interact with influencers, it's clear that they no longer view them as mere spokespeople. Today, influencers are collaborators. They co-create content that resonates with their audiences, lending a sense of authenticity that traditional advertising often lacks. This shift is crucial; it means that influence is now a two-way street. Brands benefit from the influencer's unique voice and connection with their audience, while influencers gain business opportunities and resources.

The tools and analytics at our disposal have also significantly evolved. Influencers and brands alike can now measure the impact of their content with a high degree of precision. Engagement rates, follower growth, click-through rates—all these metrics are tracked, allowing for data-driven strategies. This analytical approach ensures that the content isn't just popular but also effective in achieving specific goals.

Of course, the rise of influencers isn't without its challenges. The saturation of the market means that standing out requires more creativity and authenticity than ever before. Audiences are savvy; they're quick to spot inauthentic attempts at engagement. This has pushed influencers to evolve continually, improving their content quality and finding new ways to engage their followers.

The influence landscape continues to be transformed by emerging technologies and platforms. Virtual reality, augmented reality, and AI are beginning to play roles in how influencers create content and how audiences experience it. For example, influencers are using AR filters to make their posts more engaging and interactive. These technologies promise to further blur the lines between digital and real-life experiences.

Live streaming is another area where influence is rapidly evolving. Platforms like Twitch and TikTok Live allow influencers to interact with their audiences in real-time, creating a sense of immediacy and intimacy that's hard to replicate in pre-recorded content. This evolution compels influencers to think on their feet, making their interactions more genuine and spontaneous.

In summary, the evolution of influence is marked by increased accessibility, authenticity, and interactivity. As the internet and social media have democratized the ability to affect public opinion, the types and depths of influence have diversified. We're witnessing a landscape where anyone with a unique voice and perspective can become a significant figure, shaping trends and conversations in ways unimaginable just a few decades ago. And as technology progresses, the forms this influence takes are bound to keep changing, ensuring that this is just the latest chapter in a continually evolving story.

The Birth of the Social Media Star

The emergence of social media fundamentally altered how influence and fame are distributed in our world. In the past, few could achieve widespread recognition without the backing of major media corporations or hefty marketing machines. However, platforms like Instagram, YouTube, and TikTok have made it possible for almost anyone with a smartphone and an internet connection to amass a following. This shift has birthed a new kind of celebrity: the social media star.

Unlike traditional celebrities who often rise to fame through established pathways in film, television, or music, social media stars build their followings directly with their audiences. They create content from their bedrooms, kitchens, and backyards, offering an authenticity that resonates with viewers. This grassroots, often candid creation process allows their fans to feel a closer, more genuine connection to these stars. For a digitally-savvy teenager, this kind of content is not just relatable but also aspirational. It suggests that fame and influence are within reach, democratizing who can be a public figure.

The success stories of early social media stars, such as YouTube pioneers like Jenna Marbles and PewDiePie, illustrate how these platforms serve as fertile ground for nurturing talent. These individuals had no traditional media experience yet carved out substantial careers by sharing their unique perspectives and talents online. Their rise to fame demonstrated that audiences are hungry for more than the polished, often manufactured personas traditionally presented by Hollywood and the music industry.

As social media platforms evolved, so did the skills and strategies necessary to succeed on them. The landscape grew more sophisticated, and with it, the demands on those hoping to ride the wave of digital fame. From engaging editing techniques to understanding the nuances of each platform's algorithm, social media stars started to navigate a complex ecosystem. The most successful among them not only mastered the art of creating engaging content but also developed a keen understanding of social media trends and audience psychology.

These digital influencers are often characterized by their ability to craft narratives that integrate naturally into their daily lives. They make their followers feel like friends rather than fans. This personalized approach helps them build a loyal and engaged audience. For instance, when a makeup artist on YouTube shares their journey from a small-town life to becoming a renowned beauty guru, it doesn't just offer makeup tips; it presents a compelling narrative of personal growth and achievement.

Moreover, social media stars have leveraged a wide array of formats to captivate and expand their audiences. Video blogs (vlogs), challenges, tutorials, live streams, and collaborative projects are just a few examples of content that have proven effective. Each piece of content is a stepping stone towards greater visibility and influence. These varied formats keep audiences engaged and coming back for more, ensuring that the social media star remains relevant in an ever-changing digital environment.

One pivotal element in the rise of social media stars is the role of audience interaction and feedback. Unlike traditional celebrities who often maintain a deliberate distance from their fans, social media influencers thrive on direct communication. They read comments, reply to messages, and even take content suggestions from their followers. This two-way interaction not only strengthens the bond between influencer and audience but also helps influencers stay attuned to what their audience wants. It's a dynamic relationship that fuels the influencer's growth and evolution.

Another critical factor in the birth of social media stars is the sense of community they foster among their followers. These communities are active, vocal, and incredibly supportive. Whether it's a Facebook Group dedicated to discussing the latest videos or a Reddit thread where fans can interact, these spaces become virtual meeting places where fans can connect over shared interests. The resulting environment is one where the social media star and their followers grow together, forming a symbiotic relationship.

The advent of brand collaborations and sponsorships has added another layer to the ecosystem of social media stars. Early on, many influencers monetized their content through platform-specific ad revenue. However, as their influence grew, so did opportunities for direct partnerships with brands. These collaborations often feel more genuine to audiences compared to traditional advertisements because they're integrated into the influencer's content in a way that aligns with their persona and values. For example, a fitness influencer promoting a new brand of athletic wear can seamlessly incorporate the product into workout routines, making the endorsement feel like a natural fit.

However, it's not just about individual success. The rise of social media stars has also had broader cultural implications. In many ways, they've redefined what it means to be a celebrity in the digital age. Traditional measures of success, such as box office sales or album releases, are now complemented, if not overshadowed, by metrics like follower counts, engagement rates, and viral impact. This shift has changed the power dynamics in the entertainment and media industries, forcing traditional celebrities and their management teams to adapt to a new, digital-first paradigm.

Beyond commercial success, many social media stars use their platforms to advocate for social issues, share educational content, and inspire their audiences. This has led to the emergence of "activist influencers" who harness their reach to affect positive change. Whether it's raising awareness about mental health challenges, promoting environmental sustainability, or advocating for social justice, these influencers prove that digital fame can be leveraged for more than just personal gain. They serve as role models, showing young people that they, too, can make a significant impact through accessible means.

The birth of the social media star marks a significant turning point not just in the landscape of fame and influence but also in how we communicate, connect, and inspire one another in the digital age. It's a testament to the power of technology and creativity to elevate everyday individuals into figures of significant social and cultural influence. For teenagers today, these digital icons present a new blueprint for achieving impact and success, one post, video, and story at a time.

The trajectory of social media stars continues to evolve, reflecting broader societal trends and technological advancements. As new platforms emerge and existing ones adapt, the next generation of social media influencers will undoubtedly push the boundaries even further. Yet, at its core, the phenomenon remains a testament to the power of personal connection, authenticity, and the democratizing force of digital media.

Chapter 2:
The Mechanics of Online Fame

A t the heart of online fame lies a complex dance between technolo-gy and human nature. Algorithms and human curiosity work hand-in-hand to create viral sensations, pushing some to stardom overnight while others remain in the shadows. Social media platforms, with their ever-changing algorithms, often determine what content gets visibility and what fades into obscurity. To thrive in this digital landscape, influencers must master various strategies—knowing when to post, engaging with followers, and leveraging trends—all while stay-ing authentic. This chapter unravels these mechanics, shedding light on the unseen forces and calculated efforts that turn ordinary individ-uals into digital celebrities, and in turn, reshape the fabrics of our daily lives and societal norms.

Algorithms and Virality

In the digital age, achieving fame isn't only about talent, luck, or tim-ing. At the heart of online stardom lies the invisible hand of algo-rithms. These sophisticated sets of rules and instructions power social media platforms, determining what content gets seen and, crucially, what goes viral. As perplexing as they might seem, understanding algo-rithms is key to cracking the code of digital fame.

Algorithms function like digital gatekeepers, analyzing an immense amount of data to predict and influence user behavior. They sift through millions of posts to surface content that's most likely to engage users, considering factors such as likes, shares, comments, and viewing time. This curatorial aspect is what makes your feed feel tailored to you, full of posts you can't help but click, like, and share.

For instance, consider Instagram's algorithm. It prioritizes content from accounts that users frequently interact with, posts that get high engagement quickly, and media that seems relevant based on past behavior. It's like having a personal assistant who knows your tastes and presents you with content it thinks you'll love. Yet, for creators, this means constantly adapting to stay relevant and seen. They need to be savvy, predicting trends, engaging with followers, and tweaking their strategies as the algorithm shifts.

YouTube's recommendation engine works similarly but takes it a step further. It doesn't just show you what you might like; it leads you down a rabbit hole of endless content that keeps you watching for hours. The platform's algorithmic prowess has made stars out of ordinary people and cats alike. Creators who understand how YouTube's system rewards watch time and viewer retention can craft videos to maximize these metrics, rocketing their content into the stratosphere of virality.

When it comes to virality, timing is crucial. Algorithms often have a short attention span; they're designed to capitalize on fresh and trending content. A meme, event, or challenge can explode overnight but may fade just as quickly. The half-life of viral fame is short, making it important for influencers to capitalize on their moments in the spotlight. They must maintain consistent content output to stay relevant, constantly feeding the algorithm with new, engaging material.

Consider the case of TikTok. It's a platform built on rapid discovery and high-speed virality. TikTok's "For You" page is an endless scroll of personalized content that can make anyone famous overnight. Its recommendation algorithm values creativity, engagement, and trend participation. A well-timed video using a trending sound or participating in a popular challenge can propel an unknown creator to instant fame. What's unique about TikTok is its democratizing power; you don't need thousands of followers to go viral – just one exceptional post.

However, algorithms are not flawless. They perpetuate biases and can create echo chambers. The content you see is often what you already like and agree with, reinforcing your existing viewpoints. For teenagers navigating their formative years, this can mean a feed that's increasingly narrow and potentially misleading. It's essential to recognize this limitation and seek diverse perspectives to counteract the algorithm's tunnel vision.

Algorithms also pose ethical considerations. Social media companies design them to keep users hooked, exploiting psychological triggers to maximize time spent on their platforms. The quest for virality can sometimes push creators to produce sensational or misleading content, aiming for quick engagement rather than meaningful interaction. This creates a precarious balance between chasing clicks and maintaining authenticity.

Understanding these mechanics empowers users and creators alike. For a teen intrigued by the digital world, this knowledge can be a superpower. By decoding the algorithm, you can better navigate your online experiences, ensuring a healthier consumption of content. For aspiring influencers, algorithm literacy becomes a cornerstone of strategy, allowing them to produce effective content that resonates and spreads.

In this interconnected world, the emphasis on algorithms illustrates the profound impact of data-driven decisions. These algorithms don't just affect individual posts and videos; they shape culture, politics, and even social movements by determining what ideas gain traction. The virality of content has the power to spark widespread social change by raising awareness and rallying support for various causes.

The path to online fame is intricate and ever-evolving, guided by algorithms that we interact with daily, often without realizing their influence. Whether you're a consumer or a creator, understanding how these algorithms work is like having a map in a new world; it won't do all the work for you, but it sure makes the journey easier. The rise of the algorithmic age has redefined fame, making it more accessible but also more elusive and complex. It's a thrilling, chaotic dance between human creativity and machine intelligence, constantly redefining what it means to be famous in the digital era.

Strategies for Building an Online Presence

Ever wondered how some people explode in popularity online, while others struggle for even a smidgen of attention? Building an online presence isn't as whimsical as it might seem. It involves a blend of creativity, strategy, and consistency. If you're hoping to carve out your own corner of the internet, it's worth understanding the mechanics that go into creating online fame.

First things first, authenticity matters. In a world brimming with influencers, authenticity is your unique selling point. People are drawn to personalities who are true to themselves. Being genuine not only fosters trust but also builds a long-term loyal audience. It's like planting a tree — it grows stronger over time if its roots are deep and genuine. Don't try to mimic someone else; people can sense insincerity a mile away.

Content is king but context is queen. The type of content you create should resonate with your audience. Are you passionate about makeup tutorials or gaming? Whatever your niche, make sure your content is tailored to the platform you're using. For example, Instagram thrives on high-quality visuals, while Twitter is great for quick updates and discussions. Know your audience and give them what they want to see.

Consistency is key. Posting regularly helps keep your audience engaged and returning for more. It's rarely the first post that garners attention but the hundredth. A predictable posting schedule helps. Whether daily, bi-weekly, or weekly, choose a rhythm and stick to it. Your audience will start to anticipate your content, making your presence a part of their routine.

Engagement is a two-way street. Interacting with your followers makes them feel valued. Reply to comments, ask for opinions, and foster a sense of community. This not only boosts your visibility but also deepens your connection with your audience. Building an online presence isn't just about broadcasting; it's about conversing.

Collaboration can turbocharge your growth. Partnering with other influencers exposes you to new audiences. It's a win-win. You get to embrace their followers, and they can benefit from yours. However, ensure that your collaborators align with your brand values. A mismatched partnership can confuse your audience and dilute your authenticity.

Leverage SEO and hashtags. These are powerful tools to get your content noticed. Research trending hashtags in your niche and use them strategically. On platforms like YouTube, optimize your video titles, descriptions, and tags so they are easily searchable. SEO and hashtags are like the trail of breadcrumbs that guide people to your content.

The visual element cannot be overstressed. Humans are visual creatures. High-quality images and videos make your content more engaging and shareable. Invest time in learning basic photography and video editing skills. Even smartphone cameras today can produce stunning results if used correctly. Remember, a picture speaks a thousand words.

Monitoring analytics is incredibly useful. Most social media platforms offer insights into how your content is performing. Understanding which posts are hits and which are flops can guide your future strategies. Analyze metrics like views, likes, shares, and comments to refine your approach continually.

Don't underestimate storytelling. People love stories. Whether it's a personal anecdote or a brand narrative, compelling storytelling can set you apart. Use stories to connect on an emotional level with your audience. Share your journey, challenges, and successes. This creates a more intimate bond with your followers.

Paid promotions can offer a quick boost. Sometimes, organic reach isn't enough, especially when you're starting out. Allocating a budget for targeted ads can help you reach a broader and more targeted audience more quickly. However, keep an eye on your ROI (Return on Investment) to ensure you're getting your money's worth.

Quality over quantity is a maxim that holds true. It might be tempting to flood your feed with posts, but quality is far more important. One well-crafted post can achieve more than ten mediocre ones. Focus on producing content that adds value, entertains, or educates. Your audience will appreciate the effort and time you put into each post.

While building an online presence, don't lose sight of mental well-being. The pressure to constantly produce content can be exhausting. Burnout is a real phenomenon. Pacing yourself and taking breaks when needed is crucial for sustaining a long-term presence. After all, your audience prefers a healthy and happy you over frequent but lackluster posts.

Learning never stops. Social media trends are ever-changing, and platforms frequently update their algorithms. Stay informed about the latest trends, tools, and techniques. Attending webinars, reading blogs, and joining online communities can keep you updated and inspire new ideas.

Your journey to building an online presence is uniquely yours. There is no one-size-fits-all formula. What works for one person might not work for another. Experiment, learn from failures, and continually adapt. The digital landscape is vast and full of opportunities. Embrace the challenge, have fun, and remember why you started in the first place. Your authenticity, creativity, and perseverance are ultimately what will set you apart in the crowded online world.

Chapter 3:
Music: From Radios to Streams

The journey of music has been nothing short of revolutionary, morphing from the crackling sounds of old-time radios to instantaneous streams on digital platforms. Back in the day, families huddled around radios, waiting for their favorite tunes, while today, teens have the world of music at their fingertips, thanks to streaming services like Spotify and Apple Music. The shift didn't just change how we consume music but also who gets to influence our playlists. Influencers, with their massive followings, wield the power to make or break new tracks and artists, setting trends and creating viral hits overnight. This digital transformation has democratized music, giving independent artists a voice and dismantling traditional gatekeeping. The impact is profound, illustrating how our relationship with music continues to evolve in this fast-paced digital era.

The Transformation of the Music Industry

Once upon a time, the music industry was an untouchable monolith, dominated by a few powerful record labels and radio stations. The advent of radio became the first major technological transformation, democratizing music for the masses. Suddenly, stars were born overnight, and songs could reach the ears of millions within hours. This era gave rise to legends and chart-toppers that could dominate radio waves for weeks, if not months.

Fast forward to the late 1990s and early 2000s, and another seismic shift occurred. Enter the internet, with its ability to share vast amounts of information instantaneously. Napster and other peer-to-peer file sharing networks shook the industry to its core, introducing a new model of music consumption. Fans were no longer reliant on radio station schedules or album release dates. They could find, share, and enjoy their favorite tracks whenever they pleased, disrupting the longstanding power held by record companies.

Streaming services are the latest revolution in the music industry. Platforms like Spotify, Apple Music, and even YouTube have reshaped how we access and listen to music. Gone are the days of purchasing individual albums or waiting for a favorite song to play on the radio. Now, for a small subscription fee or even free with ads, listeners have millions of songs at their fingertips. This shift has not only changed the way music is consumed but also how it is created, distributed, and promoted.

The most interesting side of this transformation? Artists now have unprecedented control over their creative output and career trajectory. Young talent can upload a track to SoundCloud or share a music video on YouTube, potentially reaching worldwide audiences overnight. The barriers to entry have lowered dramatically, enabling a more diverse array of voices and genres to flourish.

Influencers and Social Media

While distribution channels have multiplied, the role of influencers in shaping musical tastes is impossible to ignore. Social media platforms have become hotspots for discovering new music, with influencers often acting as modern-day DJs. A single endorsement from a popular influencer can propel a song from obscurity to the top of the charts. Think about how artists like Lil Nas X and Billie Eilish initially gained massive followings through platforms like TikTok and Instagram.

Furthermore, influencers contribute more than just their endorsements. They actively engage with their communities by sharing playlists, hosting virtual listening parties, and even featuring emerging artists in their content. This new form of musical curation fosters a much more interactive and engaged fan base. When an influencer genuinely loves a song or artist, their followers are more likely to give it a listen, often creating a ripple effect.

But it's not all sunshine and rainbows. The ease of music production and distribution has also led to market saturation. It's now more challenging than ever for artists to stand out among the sea of available content. Playlists on streaming platforms are often controlled by algorithms that favor certain tracks, and breaking through those algorithmic barriers can seem like an insurmountable challenge. Here, once again, influencers play an essential role by humanizing the selection process and giving deserving artists a much-needed platform.

For today's teenagers, this transformation heralds an era of unparalleled choice and accessibility. You have the power to explore genres, cultures, and sounds from every corner of the globe. No longer constrained by traditional gatekeepers, your musical tastes can be as eclectic and personalized as you make them. The omnipresence of music in your daily life, from TikTok challenges to Spotify recommendations, allows for constant discovery and connection. This newfound accessibility can inspire budding musicians to try their hand at creating, knowing they, too, have a viable shot at being heard.

Economic Shifts

Financial models in the music industry have also experienced a significant overhaul. While traditional album sales continue to decline, revenue from streaming services has surged. Subscription models and ad-supported free tiers have shown that consumers are willing to pay for convenience and access. This change has prompted artists and labels to diversify their income streams, often focusing on live performances, merchandise, and brand partnerships to supplement their earnings.

The advent of digital distribution has also led to more equitable revenue splits. Independent artists can now bypass record labels, retaining a more substantial portion of their earnings. Platforms like Bandcamp allow musicians to sell their work directly to fans, fostering a closer artist-listener relationship. Such platforms emphasize the potential for transparency and fairness in an industry historically marred by opaque practices and exploitative contracts.

Nevertheless, challenges remain. The focus on streams and views can sometimes prioritize quantity over quality. Artists may feel pressured to churn out content to stay relevant, leading to concerns about sustainability and creative integrity. The reliance on social media algorithms can also be a double-edged sword, providing visibility one moment and drowning out voices the next. Balancing artistic expression with commercial viability continues to be an intricate dance in this transformed landscape.

Technological Innovations

Technology continues to drive these changes at a breakneck pace. Virtual reality concerts, AI-driven music production, and blockchain-based royalty tracking represent just a few of the innovations on the horizon. These advancements promise to further democratize the industry, offering new ways to experience, create, and monetize music.

Virtual reality concerts, for instance, offer a unique blend of live performance and immersive experience. Platforms like Wave and Fortnite have already hosted VR concerts, attracting millions of virtual attendees. This technology not only expands audience reach but also reduces logistical challenges and costs associated with traditional live events.

AI and machine learning are also playing a growing role in music production and curation. Tools like Amper Music and Jukedeck enable anyone, regardless of musical training, to compose tracks easily. While this raises questions about the nature of creativity, it also opens up new avenues for experimentation and collaboration. Artists can leverage AI to push the boundaries of their work, blending human ingenuity with computational prowess.

The Road Ahead

The transformation of the music industry is an ongoing journey, fueled by technological advancements and evolving consumer behaviors. For your digitally-savvy generation, this landscape offers excitement and opportunity. You hold the keys to further innovation and change, whether as listeners, creators, or curators. Embrace these shifts, experiment with new sounds, and recognize the power you have in shaping the future of music.

In this dynamic environment, staying informed and adaptable is crucial. Keep an eye on emerging trends and technologies, and don't be afraid to explore diverse musical avenues. The industry's transformation is a testament to the enduring human connection to music. It's a constantly evolving symphony, and you are both the audience and the conductors of this incredible journey.

How Influencers Shape Musical Tastes

The way we listen to music has hugely evolved over the years, shifting from the static predictability of radio to the eclectic dynamism of streaming platforms. Within this transformation, influencers have emerged as key taste-makers. They wield power not just over what music becomes popular but how it's consumed, interpreted, and embraced by teens around the world.

Influencers often possess an uncanny ability to tap into the current zeitgeist and amplify it. Social media feeds are packed with playlists, music recommendations, and spontaneous jam sessions. Whether it's a snippet of a new track on TikTok or an Instagram story featuring a behind-the-scenes look at a concert, these moments spark curiosity and lead to exploration. Teens are more likely to give a song a listen if their favorite influencer endorses it. This social validation creates a direct path from influencer to listener.

A key aspect of this influence lies in the sheer accessibility and relatability of these influencers. Unlike traditional celebrities who seem worlds apart, social media stars often initiate one-on-one interactions with their followers. When an influencer with millions of followers posts a Spotify playlist or shares a song on their Instagram story, it feels like an intimate recommendation from a friend rather than a distant announcement from an artist's management team. This democratization of music discovery has shifted power from industry gatekeepers to individual voices on social media.

Moreover, influencers don't just recommend music; they shape entire musical trends. Take the viral dance challenges on TikTok, for example. These challenges often feature specific songs that skyrocket in popularity as they're used, reused, and imitated by millions. Tracks that might have otherwise languished in obscurity find new life and chart success, thanks to the viral backing of influential accounts.

Another fascinating dimension is how influencers revive older genres and songs. With their wide reach, they possess the power to breathe new life into forgotten tracks. Consider how a single TikTok video can turn a decades-old song into an overnight sensation. This phenomenon has allowed for a more diverse musical landscape, as teens are exposed to a wider variety of sounds and styles than ever before.

Discussions about music today often go beyond the lyrics and melodies; they encompass the stories behind the songs. Influencers excel at creating these narratives. They share their personal connections to music, offering anecdotes that make songs more relatable and impactful. The story of why a song matters to an influencer can be a powerful tool in shaping its reception among followers. This storytelling is not just limited to new releases but also extends to emerging artists, giving them a platform that can be more effective than traditional media coverage.

The collaborative nature of social media further enhances this effect. Influencers can easily team up with artists for joint projects or sponsored content, which often leads to mutual growth. For example, an artist might debut a new song exclusively through an influencer's channel, blending the lines between entertainment and marketing. These collaborations can give songs a much-needed push, helping them to stand out in a saturated market.

Finally, the practice of live-streaming has introduced a fresh way for fans and followers to engage with music. Platforms like Instagram Live and Twitch allow influencers to host virtual listening parties, live performances, and Q&A sessions. These experiences create a sense of community and shared enjoyment around music. Followers don't just passively listen; they actively participate, offering their opinions in real-time and feeling like an integral part of the music discovery process.

In conclusion, influencers play an indispensable role in shaping musical tastes in today's digital age. Through relatable content, spontaneous recommendations, and powerful storytelling, they transform how teens discover and connect with music. Their impact is profound, turning mere listeners into engaged, enthusiastic fans ready to champion the next big hit.

Chapter 4:
Fashion Forward:
Trends and Tastemakers

The world of fashion has always been dynamic, but with the rise of digital platforms, it's evolving at a breakneck pace, driven largely by influencers who set the trends. These digital fashion icons, from Instagram moguls to TikTok trendsetters, wield immense power, often shaping the styles you see on the streets and in schools. They do more than just showcase outfits; they embody the aspirations and identities of their followers, turning personal brand aesthetics into global fashion statements. By leveraging social media's visual nature, these tastemakers can turn an unknown brand into the next big thing almost overnight. Their reach and impact are profound, marking a shift from traditional fashion houses dictating trends to a more democratized, inclusive landscape where anyone with a unique style and a smartphone can influence, inspire, and lead.

Influencers as Fashion Icons

In today's digital age, influencers have become synonymous with trendsetting in fashion. Their capacity to reach millions in mere seconds makes them powerful arbiters of style. A single post featuring an outfit hastily put together for a morning coffee run can inspire widespread replication before lunchtime. For a curious teenager looking to understand the dynamics of this modern phenomenon, it's essential to grasp how influencers craft their fashion narrative and the impact it has on your everyday wardrobe choices.

The role of influencers as fashion icons is multi-faceted. They are more than just models sporting the latest trends; they are storytellers, creating entire narrative arcs through their posts, videos, and stories. These narratives are not confined to runways or photo studios but extend to everyday settings like bedrooms, city streets, and cafes. This relatability makes their fashion choices feel accessible and achievable, fostering a sense of connection with their audience.

Consider the way influencers use platforms like Instagram and TikTok. The visual nature of these platforms allows for a dynamic display of outfits, often accompanied by engaging captions, behind-the-scenes looks, and short video clips. This multi-dimensional approach to presenting fashion allows followers to see clothing not just as items to be worn but as pieces in a larger lifestyle puzzle.

Inspiration from everyday settings

Engaging storytelling through captions and videos

Accessibility of fashion trends

These influencers don't just wear clothes; they personify a lifestyle. They bring fashion to life through their daily routines, travels, and social interactions. Moreover, their ability to mix high fashion with affordable brands speaks to a broader demographic, especially teenagers who may be exploring their style on a budget. By showcasing a combination of luxury items with more affordable pieces, influencers demonstrate that style is about expression, not just expenditure.

Teenagers are particularly susceptible to the fashion choices of influencers due to the relatability factor. Unlike traditional celebrities who often seem out of reach, influencers appear more like a best friend or older sibling. They share real-life moments, struggles, and successes, allowing their audience to see themselves reflected in the influencer's life. This creates a sense of authenticity and trust, making the fashion choices of influencers more impactful.

Additionally, the diversity among fashion influencers has expanded significantly in recent years. Whether it's body positivity, gender fluidity, or cultural representation, today's influencers span a wide range of identities that resonate with a diverse teenage audience. This inclusivity provides inspiration to teenagers who might not see themselves represented in traditional fashion media. Influencers have made it clear that style is universal and that anyone, regardless of their background, can be a fashion icon.

The dynamics of fondness and emulation you experience as a teenager are genuinely intriguing. The blend of aspiration and relatability makes influencers key figures in your fashion journey. They provide direct links to purchase the items they showcase, often coupled with discount codes and promotions, shattering the once opaque barrier between fashion marketing and actual consumerism. This immediacy in converting admiration into action transforms passive viewers into active participants in the fashion ecosystem.

Let's not overlook the ethical aspect that has become increasingly central to the role of fashion influencers. Many influencers are leveraging their platforms to advocate for sustainable and ethical fashion, challenging their audience to consider the impact of their clothing choices on the planet. This wave of conscious consumerism is particularly resonant with younger audiences who are more environmentally aware. It behooves teenagers like you to recognize how influencers are shaping these critical discourses and integrating them into their brand narratives.

Mixing high fashion with accessible brands

Creating authenticity through relatability

Representation and inclusivity

Advocating for sustainable fashion

Moreover, the collaboration between influencers and fashion brands has redefined marketing strategies. Instead of traditional advertisements, brands now rely on influencers to promote new lines, often resulting in sold-out collections within hours. Influencers bring a genuine endorsement that feels more personal and trustworthy. You might find yourself more inclined to purchase a product recommended by an influencer you follow and admire. This evolving marketing landscape highlights the influential power these social media figures wield.

But of course, with great power comes great responsibility. Influencers are constantly under scrutiny, both for their choices and the messages they endorse. It's essential to approach influencer-driven fashion with a critical eye. Are they promoting sustainable practices? Are they transparent about sponsored content? And most importantly, do their values align with yours? These are questions that can guide you in making more informed choices.

Fashion influencers offer a rich blend of inspiration and practical advice, making them indispensable guides in your style evolution. From casual, everyday looks to more elaborate fashion statements, they provide a roadmap that helps you navigate your own sartorial journey. Their influence extends beyond mere aesthetics, offering lessons in confidence, self-expression, and the importance of staying true to oneself.

In sum, the phenomenon of influencers as fashion icons encompasses a complex, yet fascinating, interplay of relatability, accessibility, ethical responsibility, and direct consumer engagement. As a teenager increasingly defining your identity through style, understanding the dynamics at play can empower you to make fashion choices that are both stylish and meaningful. Dive into the colorful world of influencer-driven fashion, but remember, your ultimate goal should be to cultivate a style that reflects who you are, not just who you follow.

The Role of Social Media in Fashion Trends

In today's fast-paced digital world, social media isn't just a tool for staying in touch with friends and family; it's a powerful engine driving fashion trends across the globe. From Instagram to TikTok, these platforms have transformed how styles emerge and spread, offering an unparalleled immediacy and reach that traditional media could only dream of.

Remember the last time you scrolled through Instagram and saw an influencer wearing a quirky new outfit? Within hours, that look might appear on fashion blogs, appear in YouTube haul videos, and ultimately find its way into your wardrobe. This instant dissemination can sometimes make it feel like trends are appearing out of nowhere, but in reality, they're carefully curated and propelled by individuals who possess a keen sense of style and a significant online following.

Social media has given rise to a new kind of tastemaker—one who's relatable and often far removed from the glossy pages of high-fashion magazines. Unlike traditional celebrities, social media influencers build their brands based on accessibility and engagement. They share not just their outfits, but also their lives, making their fashion choices feel all the more attainable. For teenagers, this is incredibly empowering. Suddenly, personal style is no longer dictated solely by designers and runway shows but shaped by relatable figures who could very well be your next-door neighbor.

This shift democratizes fashion. Teenagers and young adults, who once had to wait for seasonal catalogues or expensive magazines, now have a front-row seat to the latest trends, free of cost. The global nature of social media means that fashion inspiration can come from anywhere—Tokyo streetwear can influence a New Yorker, and a Parisian chic look might inspire someone in Sydney. This cultural exchange promotes a more eclectic and inclusive fashion landscape, where diverse styles and perspectives thrive.

What's fascinating is how quickly these trends can evolve. One day, everyone might be obsessing over minimalist, monochrome outfits. A week later, vibrant, neon styles can take over. The flexibility of social media platforms allows fashion trends to be as fluid as the digital space they live in. It's a double-edged sword, however; while it keeps fashion fun and dynamic, it can also create pressure to constantly stay updated, which isn't always feasible for everyone.

In addition to influencers, everyday users play a crucial role in this model. Platforms like TikTok have trending hashtags like #OOTD (Outfit of the Day) and #ThriftFlip, where users showcase their daily outfits or DIY-ed clothing items. These user-generated trends often become viral, collectively shaping the fashion landscape. It's a community-driven approach that encourages participation and creativity, making fashion a more interactive experience.

Brands have responded to this paradigm shift by aligning their marketing strategies to be more social media-centric. They collaborate with influencers for product launches and fashion lines, leveraging their reach to tap into engaged audiences. What's notable is the transparent nature of these partnerships, often disclosed with hashtags like #Ad or #Sponsored. This transparency not only maintains trust but also educates the follower base about the commercialization aspects of the content they consume.

One of the most impactful aspects of social media in driving fashion trends is the immediacy it provides for feedback. Unlike traditional fashion channels, where consumer response might come in weeks or months, social media offers almost instant reactions. A new fashion line can quickly gauge its success or failure through likes, comments, and shares. This immediate feedback loop enables designers and brands to be more responsive and adaptive, often tweaking their offerings to better suit their audience.

Moreover, the interactive nature of social media platforms encourages engagement beyond mere consumption. Platforms like Instagram and Pinterest allow users to curate their fashion boards, making them personal stylists in their own right. For teenagers, this can be incredibly fulfilling; it provides a sense of control and personal expression in a world where youth often feel unheard. Creating and sharing personal styles can build confidence and even spark budding interests in fashion design or marketing.

Interestingly, the role of social media in fashion trends goes beyond individual influencers or viral hashtags. It's also changing how fashion weeks and runway shows operate. Livestreaming these exclusive events breaks down barriers, allowing people worldwide to witness the latest designs in real-time. This transparency has shifted fashion weeks from exclusive industry events to global spectacles—democratizing access, and consumer influence like never before.

However, it's essential to remember that social media's influence on fashion goes beyond the positive. The speed at which trends evolve can create a culture of fast fashion, leading to ethical and environmental concerns. The desire to keep up with the latest trends can encourage overconsumption, contributing to waste and unsustainable practices. It's a dilemma that the fashion industry, influencers, and consumers must collectively address.

In response to these challenges, a counter-movement is also thriving—one that promotes sustainable fashion practices. Influencers advocating for thrift shopping, upcycling clothes, and supporting ethically produced garments are gaining traction. This highlights social media's potential not just to spur trends but also to foster positive change. For teenagers, this is particularly impactful, offering them a framework for making mindful fashion choices that consider the broader implications.

Ultimately, social media's role in fashion trends is multifaceted and ever-evolving. It democratizes style, amplifies diverse voices, and fosters a global fashion culture that's more interconnected than ever. For teenagers, understanding this dynamic can be both enlightening and empowering. It offers a way to engage with fashion that's active rather than passive, encouraging personal expression and ethical considerations.

By being aware of how social media shapes fashion, teens can navigate these digital waters with a blend of enthusiasm and mindfulness. They can participate in the joys of fashion dynamics while also contributing to a more sustainable and inclusive future. The next time you see a trending hashtag or an influencer's latest post, remember you're participating in a vast, collaborative network that's redefining fashion—one post at a time.

Chapter 5:
Film and Television:
Influencers on Screen

The way YouTube stars and other online influencers have permeated film and television is nothing short of remarkable. Once relegated to the fringes of entertainment, these digital creators now boast mainstream appeal, translating their online personas into TV shows, movies, and even hosting gigs on major networks. Influencers like Lilly Singh and Liza Koshy have not only crossed over; they've brought their unique style and massive audiences with them, challenging traditional media to rethink its boundaries. It's fascinating to see how these modern-day influencers utilize their cross-platform popularity to build multimedia empires, blending personal branding with large-scale production. Their success stories inspire aspiring creators, reinforcing the idea that new media can coexist with—and even rejuvenate—traditional film and television. This synergy between digital influence and mainstream media marks a significant shift in how we consume entertainment, showing that the screen is big enough to encompass creators from all walks of life.

The Power of the YouTube Star

The world of film and television has been irrevocably altered by the rise of YouTube stars. These influencers, who began creating content with little more than a camera and a big idea, have transitioned from screens on laptops and phones to starring roles in major film and television productions. But what makes a YouTube star so powerful? And how have they managed to cross the barrier into mainstream media?

One of the most striking aspects of YouTube stars is their ability to cultivate a deeply personal connection with their audience. Unlike traditional celebrities, who often seem distant and untouchable, YouTubers engage with their fans in real-time, responding to comments, making Q&A videos, and sharing intimate details of their lives. This authenticity renders them relatable and trustworthy, which is a goldmine for producers looking to tap into pre-existing fanbases. When a YouTube star steps onto a different screen, they bring with them a loyal following that can translate into higher ratings and ticket sales.

Consider the case of Lilly Singh, also known as *Superwoman* on YouTube. She amassed millions of followers through her comedic skits and relatable content. Her genuine personality and unique style caught the attention of television execs, leading to her own late-night talk show on NBC, *A Little Late with Lilly Singh*. This transition exemplifies the power dynamic at play: YouTube stars offer guaranteed viewership from their already established audiences, making them highly attractive candidates for traditional media roles.

But it's not just the existing fanbase that makes a YouTube star powerful. Their innate understanding of digital culture and trends is invaluable. YouTube creators are storytellers who have honed their craft in an arena where audience feedback is instantaneous and brutal. They know how to capture attention within seconds, keep viewers engaged, and adapt content according to trending topics. This skill set translates well to film and television, where capturing and maintaining viewer interest is the ultimate goal.

Additionally, YouTubers often have a multifaceted skill set that extends beyond just their on-camera personas. They are often involved in scriptwriting, editing, marketing, and even the technical aspects of production. This versatility makes them well-suited to the demands of film and television production, where collaborative and well-rounded talent is always in high demand. For example, Issa Rae, who started with her YouTube series *The Misadventures of Awkward Black Girl*, went on to create and star in the critically acclaimed HBO show *Insecure*. Rae's ability to wear multiple hats not only enhanced her own projects but also illustrated the diverse skill sets YouTubers bring to the table.

Beyond their technical skills, YouTube stars are trailblazers when it comes to content innovation. They're unafraid to experiment with unconventional formats and narratives, often pushing the boundaries of what traditional media deems acceptable. Their success online provides them with a platform to advocate for more inclusive and varied representations on-screen. It's not uncommon for YouTube stars to leverage their popularity to push for more diverse casting and storytelling in the projects they undertake in traditional media. They bring new voices and perspectives, enriching the cultural landscape of film and television.

Another example of a successful YouTuber making the leap to traditional media is Grace Helbig. Initially gaining fame through her channel *It's Grace*, she parlayed her internet popularity into a television show on E!, aptly named *The Grace Helbig Show*, and starred in several films. Helbig's laid-back, witty persona translated well to mainstream media, showcasing how a strong personal brand can transcend into different platforms. It's a clear indicator of how YouTube stars not only adapt but thrive in the traditional entertainment ecosystem.

It's also worth mentioning that YouTube stars often bring a level of creative control and independence that is refreshing to the traditional media world. Used to producing and directing their own content, they often demand more creative freedom in film and television projects. This shift is challenging established norms and fostering a new kind of collaboration where ideas flow more freely. The result?

Content that is fresher, more dynamic, and deeply resonant with younger audiences.

However, the journey from YouTube to mainstream stardom isn't without its challenges. Not every YouTube sensation makes a seamless transition. The format and pacing of online videos are starkly different from those of films and television shows. While YouTube videos thrive on quick cuts, high energy, and a DIY aesthetic, traditional media often requires a more polished and paced approach. Adapting to these differences can be a significant hurdle for some YouTubers. Nonetheless, the ones who succeed bring a renewed vibrancy to the film and television landscape.

Furthermore, the rise of YouTube stars in mainstream media has altered the way traditional stars engage with their audiences. Celebrities are now seen regularly creating YouTube channels to stay relevant and maintain a connection with their fans. This cross-pollination illustrates just how influential YouTube stars have become. The merging of these realms signifies a new era in entertainment where the lines between online and offline fame are increasingly blurred.

In conclusion, the power of the YouTube star in film and television is profound. They bring a fresh, authentic voice, an engaged audience, technical skills, and creative innovation. Their influence is pushing boundaries and redefining what it means to be a star in the modern age. As these digital creators continue to make their mark, they'll undoubtedly shape the future of film and television in ways we've only just begun to understand.

Cross-Platform Popularity

In today's digital age, the boundary between traditional media and online platforms is increasingly blurred. You've probably noticed how your favorite YouTubers are showing up not just on your phone screens, but also on TV, in movies, and even in advertisements all over social media. This merger of screen time demonstrates the phenomenon of cross-platform popularity, where influencers seamlessly navigate between different media to maximize their reach and impact.

Historically, fame was a one-dimensional concept – a movie star was a movie star, and a TV actor stayed within the bounds of television. However, the rise of social media has democratized fame, allowing influencers to gain quick access to multiple platforms, each with its unique audience. Take Lilly Singh, for instance. She started on YouTube as "Superwoman," amassing millions of followers with her comedic sketches. This popularity led to her hosting her own late-night TV show. Her ability to transition from one platform to another highlights the dynamic nature of modern-day influencing.

One of the most remarkable aspects of cross-platform popularity is its inclusivity. Whether you're into comedy, makeup tutorials, or video game streaming, there's a niche – and a platform – for everyone. This diversity is not only appealing but also creates vast opportunities for influencers to broaden their horizons. Imagine a Twitch streamer who's just launched a podcast on Spotify, or a TikToker who's now collaborating with a major clothing brand for a TV ad. These individuals command different platforms, yet they harmonize their content in a way that feels seamless and organic.

Cross-platform success often hinges on an influencer's ability to remain authentic while adapting to the nuances of each platform. Authenticity builds trust, and trust keeps audiences coming back for more. For example, someone who follows a makeup artist on YouTube probably also appreciates their candid Instagram Stories or live streams on Twitch. Authenticity becomes the glue that binds an influencer's multi-platform presence.

Interactivity also plays a crucial role in cross-platform popularity. Social media platforms thrive on interaction, whether it's through likes, comments, shares, or other forms of engagement. Influencers who can effectively engage their audience across multiple platforms often see exponential growth. A good example is Emma Chamberlain, who utilizes her YouTube channel to create long-form content while using Instagram for daily updates and Twitter for personal musings. This cross-platform strategy keeps her fans constantly engaged, no matter where they tune in.

It's not just individual influencers who benefit from cross-platform popularity; entire brands have tapped into this trend too. Consider how Netflix uses Instagram to promote its latest releases or how major films have teaser trailers debuting on YouTube. These tactics aren't just about advertising; they're about creating an ecosystem where each platform serves a unique purpose in a broader promotional strategy.

Different platforms provide different lenses through which fans can view their favorite influencers. Each social media platform has its strengths – YouTube offers in-depth content, TikTok provides quick and entertaining clips, Instagram allows for visually stunning posts, and Twitter gives a space for instant reactions. By leveraging these strengths, influencers don't just reach a wider audience; they offer varied experiences to their followers, enriching their overall engagement.

The economics of cross-platform popularity can also be compelling. The synergy of multiple platforms allows influencers to diversify their revenue streams. On YouTube, they may earn through ad revenue and sponsorships, while on Instagram, brand partnerships and sponsored posts can be lucrative. Twitch might bring in income through subscriptions and donations. This multi-pronged approach not only maximizes income potential but also provides stability should one platform's algorithms or policies change unexpectedly.

Another critical element is the role of collaborations and cross-promotions. Influencers often collaborate across platforms, bringing together their audiences for mutual benefit. A YouTuber might feature a popular TikToker in a video, and in turn, appear in that Tik-Toker's content. These collaborations ignite a cross-platform synergy that can introduce each influencer to new followers, boosting their popularity further.

Cross-platform strategies also make influencers more resilient to platform-specific issues. If an algorithm change on one platform suddenly reduces their reach, they still have their audience on other platforms. This resiliency ensures that their influence remains strong and more stable in the fluctuating digital landscape.

Moreover, cross-platform popularity often leads to greater mainstream recognition. Influencers who started on YouTube or TikTok might find themselves invited to talk shows, award events, and traditional media outlets, further cementing their status as public figures. This mainstream crossover also serves as validation, bridging the gap between internet fame and conventional celebrity status.

As technology continues to evolve, so does the potential for cross-platform engagement. Virtual reality (VR) and augmented reality (AR) are opening new horizons for interactive, immersive experiences. Imagine watching a VR concert by a musician you discovered on Spotify or exploring a movie set in AR featuring your favorite Instagrammer. These emerging technologies will further enrich the cross-platform ecosystem, providing even more avenues for engagement and influence.

In essence, cross-platform popularity isn't just a trend; it's a paradigm shift in how fame is attained and maintained. For today's digital-savvy teenager, understanding this concept isn't just fascinating—it's essential. It reveals the limitless possibilities available to those who can blend creativity with tech-savvy, turning passion into a multi-platform career. Influencers on screen aren't just shaping the present; they're crafting the future of entertainment across every platform.

Chapter 6:
The Power of Social Media
Platforms

In an era where sharing, following, and liking are second nature, social media platforms hold immense power in shaping pop culture and influencer dynamics. It's not just about posting a picture or a video; it's about how these platforms amplify voices, dictate trends, and build massive communities. A single viral post on TikTok or a meticulously curated Instagram feed can reach millions, driving cultural phenomena almost overnight. These platforms are not only tools for entertainment and connection but also engines of significant social influence. The unique algorithms and features of each platform create distinct types of engagement and opportunities, making it possible for influencers to shape public discourse, fashion trends, musical tastes, and even social movements. By understanding the strengths and idiosyncrasies of these digital spaces, teenagers can better navigate and influence a fast-evolving social landscape.

Understanding Each Platform

Social media platforms have become the beating heart of modern communication and culture. They're not just tools; they're dynamic spaces that shape everything from conversations to trends. Each platform has its own unique characteristics, vibes, and communities, which is why understanding them is crucial for anyone looking to navigate the digital world effectively.

To start, let's consider Facebook. Once the reigning king of social media, it's now more like a digital scrapbook for many users. Facebook's strength lies in its versatility. You can share long posts, upload videos, join groups, and even buy and sell goods. Its algorithm prioritizes content from friends and family but also serves up a hearty mix of advertisements and sponsored posts. This mix can influence what you think, what you buy, and even how you feel, as the platform caters increasingly personalized content to you.

Then there's Twitter, the fast-paced, real-time conversation hub. Think of Twitter as the modern-day public square, where news breaks and trends emerge in a matter of minutes. The platform's 280-character limit forces brevity and wit, making it a fertile ground for memes, breaking news, and quick updates. But it's also home to nuanced discussions, activism, and sometimes contentious debates. An essential aspect to consider is Twitter's use of hashtags and trending topics, which can amplify voices and messages in a way that few other platforms can.

Instagram offers a visual feast. Initially just a photo-sharing app, it's become a cultural behemoth, influencing everything from fashion to food. With features like Stories, IGTV, and Reels, Instagram combines several formats to keep its audience engaged. The platform's focus on visual content makes it a perfect playground for influencers and brands. High-quality photos, creative videos, and aesthetically pleasing feeds can catapult an individual's status to that of a digital superstar, practically overnight.

And we can't talk about video without mentioning YouTube. YouTube isn't just a video-sharing site; it's a launchpad for careers. It has been pivotal for numerous influencers who have transitioned from screen-to-screen fame. Whether it's your favorite daily vlogger, a makeup tutorial guru, or an educational channel, YouTube has a broad spectrum of content that appeals to almost every possible interest. Its extensive recommendation algorithm can keep viewers glued to their screens for hours, quickly turning casual viewers into dedicated fans.

Snapchat pioneered the concept of ephemeral content—snaps and stories that disappear after 24 hours. This temporary nature encourages spontaneity and authenticity. It's a platform that's particularly popular among younger audiences who value the in-the-moment vibe. Snapchat's various fun filters and lenses have also set trends that spill over into other platforms. Even though its spotlight has somewhat dimmed with the rise of Instagram and TikTok, Snapchat remains a key player among teens and young adults.

Speaking of TikTok, this relatively new player has taken the world by storm. TikTok is all about short-form video content that is engaging, often funny, and incredibly shareable. Its algorithm is phenomenal at surfacing content based on your interaction patterns, which means new trends can go viral in an astonishingly short amount of time. Whether it's dance challenges, DIY hacks, or quick comedic skits, Tik-Tok offers something for everyone and has proven to be a breeding ground for the next generation of influencers.

LinkedIn might seem like the odd one out in a list mainly made up of platforms known for entertainment, but it has its own crucial role. A professional networking site at its core, LinkedIn is invaluable for career building and industry insights. Influencers on LinkedIn are often thought leaders, CEOs, and professionals who share their experiences, insights, and sometimes, their day-to-day work life. It's a great platform for learning and professional growth, and it shows how influence isn't limited to just pop culture, but also thrives in corporate and professional environments.

Let's not overlook Pinterest, the digital mood board. Pinterest excels at aggregating ideas and inspiration. From fashion tips to DIY projects, recipes to interior design, if you can think of it, you can probably find a "pin" for it. Its visual-centric, searchable format makes it an excellent tool for people looking to discover new trends and ideas, influencing everything from wedding planning to home renovations.

Reddit, often referred to as "the front page of the internet," is a unique beast altogether. It hosts countless communities (called subreddits) dedicated to virtually every topic imaginable. Reddit thrives on user-generated content and community engagement, offering deep discussions, niche communities, and upvoting/downvoting mechanisms that help the best content rise to the top. It's a platform that fosters deep dives into specific interests and is instrumental for movements and trends within its highly engaged user base.

Finally, platforms like Twitch take social interaction and turn it into a live performance. Originally focused on gaming, Twitch now hosts live streams on just about any topic, from cooking to music performances. It's a place where fans can interact with their favorite streamers in real time, fostering a unique sense of community and connection. Donations, subscriptions, and bits add an element of financial support, making it another avenue where influencers can monetize their content.

Understanding these platforms is just the first step in leveraging them effectively. Each offers various strategies and opportunities for engagement, influence, and even revenue generation. While platforms may overlap in some features, each has its unique strengths and weaknesses that shape the kind of content that thrives on them. This intricate ecosystem is why some influencers can cross from one platform to another effortlessly, while others find their niche and stick to it.

The digital landscape is ever-evolving, and staying ahead means not just using these platforms but mastering what each does best. By appreciating these nuances, a digitally-savvy teenager can better understand how to navigate their digital lives, become informed about the influence they absorb, and perhaps even create a wave of influence themselves.

The Rise of TikTok and Instagram

When you think about social media today, it's hard to overlook the monumental presence of TikTok and Instagram. These platforms have not only revolutionized how we interact online but have fundamentally changed pop culture and influencer dynamics. Unlike earlier social media giants, TikTok and Instagram offer unique experiences that cater to the fast-paced, visually-driven preferences of modern teens.

In just a few years, TikTok has exploded in popularity, becoming a global phenomenon. What makes TikTok especially captivating is its simple yet powerful algorithm. It delivers an endless stream of content tailored to your interests, making it highly addictive. The platform's short-form video format challenges creators to capture attention quickly, leading to innovative, bite-sized pieces of entertainment. Whether it's dance challenges, comedy skits, or educational content, TikTok's diversity in content keeps users hooked for hours on end.

Instagram, while older, has consistently evolved to maintain its relevance. Originally launched as a simple photo-sharing app, Instagram has integrated a variety of new features like Stories, IGTV, and Reels, trying to keep pace with the growing demand for video content inspired by TikTok's success. These features allow influencers and everyday users alike to share snippets of their lives in more dynamic ways than static photos could ever offer.

The rise of these platforms has democratized fame in unprecedented ways. In the past, achieving celebrity status required connections, luck, and often, significant financial resources. But Instagram and TikTok enable anyone with a smartphone and a creative idea to reach millions. Take Charli D'Amelio, for instance, who skyrocketed to fame through her dance videos on TikTok. Unlike traditional celebrities, her journey to stardom was fueled by relatability and the viral nature of TikTok's algorithm.

Instagram, on the other hand, has nurtured a different kind of influencer—the aesthetic curator. Here, success often hinges on maintaining a visually cohesive, aspirational lifestyle. Influencers use meticulously planned photo feeds to showcase their personal brands. From fashion and fitness to travel and food, these curated profiles offer a window into idealized versions of life, capturing the imagination and envy of millions.

Both platforms have become essential tools for brand marketing. Companies now allocate significant portions of their advertising budgets to influencer collaborations. The reason? Influencers on TikTok and Instagram can connect with audiences in ways that traditional ads can't. A sponsored post or a brand partnership feels more like a recommendation from a friend rather than a hard sell. This subtlety makes the marketing immensely effective and often leads to higher engagement rates.

However, it's important to acknowledge the challenges that come with the rapid rise of these social media giants. The pressure to constantly produce engaging content can be overwhelming, leading to burnout for many creators. Additionally, because both platforms thrive on algorithms that prioritize the most engaging content, there's an inherent risk of promoting superficiality over genuine connection. This can perpetuate unrealistic standards and fuel a cycle of comparison and self-doubt among young users.

Nevertheless, the benefits continue to draw millions to these platforms. TikTok's rise, in particular, has sparked a renewed appreciation for creativity and self-expression. It's a place where dance routines can go viral overnight, where educational content can reach massive audiences, and where social movements find their voice. The platform's unique blend of entertainment and education has made it a powerful force in shaping cultural trends.

Instagram, too, offers more than just a highlight reel of someone's best moments. With features like Stories and Live, it allows for more spontaneous and genuine interactions. This has given rise to a new breed of influencers who prioritize authenticity over perfection. By sharing the highs and lows of their lives, these influencers foster a deeper connection with their audience, creating communities that feel more like supportive circles of friends rather than fans.

Looking at the broader scope, the rise of TikTok and Instagram highlights a significant shift in the landscape of social media. These platforms epitomize the move towards visual and short-form content, reflecting the evolving tastes and attention spans of today's youth. They also emphasize the importance of adaptability in the digital age, as both platforms continuously evolve to meet user demands and stay ahead of competitors.

In essence, TikTok and Instagram have reshaped the way we perceive influence and fame. They've lowered the barriers to entry, making it possible for anyone to become a star from the comfort of their bedroom. And while this democratization of fame presents new challenges, it also opens up a world of opportunities for creative expression and community building. For today's digitally-savvy teens, mastering these platforms can be a gateway to understanding and navigating the intricate world of modern pop culture.

As we continue to explore the power of social media platforms, it becomes evident that the influence of TikTok and Instagram extends far beyond their digital interfaces. They impact fashion trends, shape musical tastes, and even influence societal norms. These platforms are not just tools for entertainment; they are the new frontier for cultural dialogue and personal expression. With every scroll, like, and share, users are actively participating in the ever-evolving story of social media's role in our lives.

In the grand narrative of social media, TikTok and Instagram stand as towering giants, each with its unique strengths and challenges. They have not just captured our attention but have transformed how we communicate, create, and connect. And as these platforms continue to grow and innovate, they'll undoubtedly continue to shape the cultural and social landscapes of tomorrow.

Chapter 7:
The Economics of Influence

Money talks, and in the world of influencers, it's got a lot to say. The economics of influence isn't just about how much cash an influencer can rake in; it's about understanding the intricate web of monetization strategies that power this digital era. Paid partnerships, sponsorships, and brand collaborations can turn a simple social media post into a goldmine. Why do big brands throw money at influencers? Because they bridge the gap between products and loyal consumers, adding a personal touch that traditional ads can't achieve. This monetization goes beyond just financial gain; it's a complex dance where influencers must balance authenticity with profitability. Teenagers scrolling through their feeds might see a glamorous life, but behind each post is a calculated strategy for engagement and revenue. The real artistry lies in making it all look effortless while navigating ever-changing algorithms and market demands.

Monetizing Influence

The world of influencing isn't just about gaining followers and spreading messages; it's also about turning that influence into income. The capacity to monetize one's online presence has transformed social media from a casual pastime into a lucrative career. But how do influencers transform likes, follows, and retweets into actual money? The answer lies in understanding the various revenue streams available and how to strategically harness them.

One of the most straightforward ways influencers monetize their presence is through sponsorships. Brands are constantly on the lookout for influencers who align with their image and values. Once a partnership is established, influencers get paid to promote products or services, often by sharing personal experiences with the brand's offerings. This kind of marketing works because followers tend to trust recommendations from people they admire. Influencers must maintain authenticity to avoid being perceived as mere advertisers, which could undermine their credibility.

Affiliate marketing is another significant source of income. Here, influencers partner with brands to promote products and receive a commission for every sale made through their unique links or promo codes. This setup benefits both parties—brands gain exposure and potential sales, while influencers earn a cut without the need for a traditional salary. Such collaborations can be long-term or just for specific campaigns, maximizing flexibility for both the brand and the influencer.

Merchandising has also become a popular way for influencers to monetize their brand. Personal merchandise—whether it's clothing, accessories, or even digital products—offers an additional revenue stream. Fans love to own items that make them feel closer to their idols, and exclusive merchandise can generate substantial income. Success in this arena often depends on an influencer's ability to tap into their community's interests and preferences, making products that are both meaningful and desirable.

Subscriptions and exclusive content provide yet another monetization avenue. Platforms like Patreon or OnlyFans allow influencers to charge for access to premium content. This might include behind-the-scenes footage, early access to posts, or specialized advice. Such content often appeals to super-fans willing to pay extra for a more intimate connection with the influencer. This model requires influencers to consistently produce high-quality, engaging content to maintain and grow their subscriber base.

Influencers also tap into ad revenue generated by the platforms they use. On YouTube, for example, influencers earn money through ads played before, during, or after their videos. The more views a video gets, the more revenue it generates. TikTok and Instagram are increasingly offering similar compensation models, allowing influencers to monetize their content directly through the platform.

Hosting events, whether virtual or physical, can bring in significant income as well. Influencers can organize meet-and-greets, virtual classes, or exclusive parties where tickets are sold to their followers. These events not only provide a direct revenue stream but also deepen the influencer's relationship with their community, fostering loyalty and increasing future earning potential.

The emergence of digital products and services offers influencers new ways to monetize. Whether creating an online course or writing an eBook, leveraging their expertise can be highly profitable. These products are often scalable, meaning they can be sold indefinitely without significant additional effort, providing a steady stream of passive income.

Syndication is an option for influencers with a large amount of high-quality content. This involves licensing their content to other platforms or media companies. By allowing others to use or distribute their content, influencers can earn money while reaching new audiences. This requires negotiating deals that ensure they receive fair compensation and retain control over how their content is used.

The expanding landscape of monetizing influence is not without its challenges. One such challenge is balancing the need for income with genuine engagement. Over-monetization can lead to follower fatigue and skepticism, reducing the influencer's long-term earning potential. Transparency and authenticity remain crucial for maintaining trust and loyalty among followers.

Furthermore, influencers must navigate the complexities of different platforms' monetization rules and algorithms. Each platform has its own set of requirements and limitations, making it essential for influencers to stay informed and adaptable. This means consistently analyzing performance metrics to optimize their content strategy and maximize earnings.

Another critical aspect is diversification. Relying on a single income stream can be risky, especially given the volatile nature of social media trends and platform policies. By diversifying income sources – for example, combining ad revenue, sponsorships, merchandise, and paid content – influencers can achieve greater financial stability.

The ability to monetize influence effectively often hinges on personal branding. Influencers need a clear, consistent, and relatable brand identity that resonates with their target audience. This involves careful curation of both content and public image, ensuring that every post, tweet, or video aligns with their brand values and messaging.

It's also important to consider the legal and financial implications of influencing as a career. Influencers must understand the tax obligations related to different forms of income and navigate contracts for sponsorships and collaborations. Legal pitfalls can be minimized by consulting with professionals, such as accountants and lawyers, who specialize in the influencer economy.

Education and continuous learning are crucial for staying ahead in the fast-paced world of influencing. Understanding market trends, consumer behavior, and new monetization technologies can provide a competitive edge. Many successful influencers invest time and resources in workshops, online courses, and industry conferences to refine their skills and strategies.

At its core, monetizing influence is about leveraging one's unique position and relationship with an audience to create value. This value can take many forms, but it always centers on the connection between the influencer and their followers. Maintaining that connection requires authenticity, creativity, and a deep understanding of both self and audience. By mastering these elements, influencers can turn their online presence into a sustainable, rewarding career.

The future of influencer monetization looks promising, with technology continually evolving to offer new opportunities. Virtual reality, for example, could revolutionize how influencers create and share content, providing even more ways to engage and monetize. Staying knowledgeable about these emerging trends will be key to future success in the field of digital influence.

Sponsorships and Brand Collaborations

In the world of digital influencers, sponsorships and brand collaborations aren't just about flashy ads or clickbait content. They represent a dynamic and ever-evolving ecosystem where cultural trends, business savvy, and consumer trust intersect. For many influencers, these collaborations are the lifeblood of their monetization strategies, allowing them to turn passion projects into sustainable careers.

Imagine your favorite YouTuber unboxing the latest smartphone. They gush about its features, showcase its capabilities, and end with a discount code just for you. As a digitally-savvy teenager, this probably resonates more than a traditional TV commercial would. And that's the magic of influencer-brand partnerships. They leverage the trust and authenticity that influencers have cultivated with their audience to create more impactful, relatable, and effective promotional content.

The appeal for brands is clear. Traditional advertising methods, like TV commercials and magazine ads, often struggle to connect with younger audiences who live in a world of ad-blockers and streaming services. Enter influencers. They not only reach these elusive demographics but engage with them on a personal level. This engagement translates to higher conversion rates and brand loyalty.

This is all part of a broader shift in advertising strategies. Brands are increasingly investing in influencer collaborations because they see higher ROI through these personalized marketing campaigns. Unlike generic advertisements, influencer endorsements come with a personal touch. This creates an emotional connection, making it more likely for their followers to try the recommended products or services.

From a teen influencer's perspective, brand collaborations can be a double-edged sword. On one hand, they offer significant financial rewards and the chance to work with cool products or companies. On the other hand, there's a fine line to walk between authentic content and blatant promotion. Losing credibility or being seen as a "sellout" can be career-damaging. Transparency and honesty are key. Most successful influencers maintain their authenticity by only promoting products they genuinely like or use.

Let's break down how these sponsorships typically work. There are different types of collaborations, ranging from sponsored posts and product placements to larger-scale partnerships like brand ambassadorships. Sponsored posts are straightforward: a brand pays the influencer to post about their product. This can include photos on Instagram, tweets, or even TikTok videos. Product placements are more subtle, where a product is featured in the content but isn't necessarily the focus.

Brand ambassadorships are more involved. They often require the influencer to commit to a series of posts or campaigns over a longer period. In return, the influencer receives compensation, which could be monetary or in the form of free products. This type of partnership creates a more consistent brand presence and can foster a deeper connection between the influencer's audience and the brand.

Authenticity remains a cornerstone of effective sponsorships. Viewers today are incredibly savvy and can spot inauthentic endorsements from miles away. Influencers who genuinely incorporate products into their lifestyle and content often see better engagement. It's this blend of authenticity and commercial viability that can make or break these collaborations.

Success stories abound in this space. Take, for instance, a makeup influencer who regularly collaborates with beauty brands. Their audience trusts their expertise and values their opinions. When they recommend a new eyeshadow palette, it can lead to a significant spike in sales. But the real triumph lies in the trust built over time, where followers feel that the recommendations are genuine and not just paid promotions.

On the flip side, poorly executed sponsorships can lead to backlash. Influencers who promote products that don't align with their personal brand or values risk alienating their audience. Think of the controversy that arises when a fitness influencer promotes unhealthy snacks. Such mismatched sponsorships can erode trust and harm both the influencer's and the brand's reputation.

The landscape is not without its ethical questions. With great influence comes great responsibility, and influencers must navigate these waters carefully. Transparency about sponsored content is crucial, and many platforms now require influencers to disclose paid partnerships. This not only maintains trust with their audience but also complies with advertising regulations.

However, the blending of personal life and advertising raises questions about consumer manipulation and the authenticity of online interactions. It challenges both influencers and audiences to maintain a critical eye on the content being consumed and promoted. For influencers, it's a balancing act of staying true to themselves while delivering value to their sponsors.

Technological advancements have also reshaped how sponsorships and collaborations operate. Analytics tools allow influencers to demonstrate their reach and engagement metrics to brands, making it easier to secure partnerships. These tools also help influencers understand their audience better, enabling more targeted and effective promotional strategies.

Emerging platforms like TikTok have introduced new dimensions to brand collaborations. With its short-form video content and highly engaged user base, TikTok has become a fertile ground for innovative sponsorship ideas. Hashtag challenges, branded effects, and collaborative content with other TikTok influencers are just a few examples of how brands can tap into the app's virality.

Ultimately, the economics of influence underlined by sponsorships and brand collaborations embody the intersection of cultural trends and commerce. They reflect how deeply embedded influencers have become in the marketing strategies of modern businesses. For young aspiring influencers, understanding this dynamic is crucial. It guides not only how they approach potential partnerships but also how they maintain their authenticity and connection with their audience.

Sponsorships and brand collaborations aren't just business transactions. They're cultural exchanges that shape and reflect the ever-changing landscape of digital engagement and consumer behavior. As this ecosystem continues to evolve, so too will the strategies and practices that define successful influencer-brand partnerships. For teens looking to make their mark, mastering the art of these collaborations could be the key to transforming influence into meaningful impact.

Chapter 8:
Diversity and Representation in Pop Culture

In a world where media images can shape perceptions and aspirations, diversity and representation in pop culture aren't just buzzwords—they're essential for societal progress. From groundbreaking shows and movies to influential social media voices, diverse representation helps dismantle stereotypes and offers everyone the chance to see themselves reflected positively. It empowers marginalized communities, fosters empathy, and broadens the perspectives of all audiences. With pop culture being a mirror that reflects societal values and norms, having inclusive depictions means challenging the status quo and championing equity. As teens, you're in a unique position to demand more inclusive content and to support creatives who are pushing boundaries and amplifying underrepresented voices. This chapter dives into how these pioneering voices are not only transforming the media landscape but also inspiring real-world change, encouraging you to think critically about the media you consume and the messages it sends.

Pioneering Voices

In the ever-expansive world of pop culture, some voices echo louder than others, especially when they break traditional molds and defy expectations. "Pioneering Voices," as it pertains to diversity and representation, is about the influencers and creatives who fight against the status quo, making way for new narratives and perspectives. These are the people who refuse to stay silent, who amplify marginalized voices, and who use their platforms to demand a more inclusive world.

Historically, mainstream media has often sidelined or misrepresented minority groups. However, pioneering voices in pop culture are rewriting these narratives. By championing diversity, they not only provide a more accurate reflection of society but also inspire countless individuals to see the value in their own stories. When we talk about pioneering voices, it's vital to highlight their role in pushing boundaries and challenging stereotypes.

Take, for instance, the influential figures in the film and television industry. Actors like Laverne Cox and Riz Ahmed have not just taken on roles that defy stereotypes but have also worked behind the scenes to advocate for more inclusive casting and storytelling. Laverne Cox, the first transgender person to be nominated for an Emmy, has become a powerful advocate for the LGBTQ+ community. Her work goes beyond just her roles; it includes her activism and public speaking, which aim to elevate transgender voices and issues.

In music, artists like Lizzo and BTS have shattered numerous barriers. Lizzo's unabashed celebration of body positivity and self-love has redefined beauty standards and encouraged countless fans to embrace their true selves. BTS, with their global appeal, have used their platform to address mental health, self-acceptance, and even social issues, reaching a diverse fan base worldwide.

Another aspect worth acknowledging is the role of social media influencers in highlighting diversity. Platforms like Instagram, YouTube, and TikTok have democratized fame, allowing underrepresented groups to find their niche audiences. Content creators such as beauty influencer Jackie Aina use their platforms not just for personal gain but to critique and call out the beauty industry's lack of inclusivity.

Jackie's advocacy for darker skin tones has led to changes within the industry, seeing the launch of more inclusive makeup lines.

The impact of pioneering voices extends beyond entertainment, affecting social norms and public discourse. Today, conversations around race, gender, and sexuality are more prominent, thanks in part to influencers who refuse to conform to outdated norms. These dialogues encourage viewers and followers to think critically about the media they consume and the systemic issues that influence it.

Pioneering voices also create a ripple effect in other sectors such as fashion. Models like Halima Aden, who became the first hijab-wearing model, challenge traditional beauty norms within the fashion industry. Her presence on and off the runway sends a powerful message about acceptance and inclusion. Fashion influencers, by showcasing diverse looks and styles, encourage a generation to embrace their unique identities.

It's not just individuals but also collaborative efforts that drive change. Content collectives and community groups are instrumental in amplifying underrepresented voices. For instance, online communities that focus on Black creators, LGBTQ+ artists, or other marginalized groups foster a sense of belonging and provide platforms for their members' creative expressions. These collectives often pave the way for mainstream recognition, bringing attention to talents that might otherwise go unnoticed.

Digital platforms play a critical role in this ecosystem. They offer the tools for pioneering voices to share their stories and connect with like-minded individuals across the globe. Hashtags like #BlackLivesMatter, #LoveIsLove, and #MeToo have become rallying cries that unite millions, illustrating that the personal is indeed political. These digital movements harness the power of pioneering voices to drive real-world change.

Moreover, these pioneers often face significant pushback and criticism. Challenging entrenched norms is rarely straightforward, and the journey is fraught with obstacles. Yet, it's their resilience and determination that set them apart. By persistently pushing boundaries, they eventually shift the cultural landscape, making it more inclusive and reflective of diverse experiences.

Education and representation also go hand in hand. Seeing diverse figures in pop culture provides critical learning opportunities for everyone. It encourages young people to explore different cultures, histories, and perspectives, promoting empathy and understanding. When students can see themselves represented, it validates their own experiences and aspirations.

At the heart of it, pioneering voices in pop culture underscore the importance of authenticity. Authenticity resonates because it's rare. In an industry often characterized by artifice and image-crafting, genuine representation stands out. These influencers succeed because they're not trying to fit into a predefined mold—they're creating new ones.

So, take a moment to appreciate and support these pioneering voices. Follow their journeys, share their content, and join the conversation. By doing so, you'll be contributing to a larger movement that values diversity and representation in ways that are meaningful and impactful. Now, imagine the kind of world you'd like to see. One where everyone has a voice and a platform. Thanks to these pioneers, we're getting closer to that reality each day.

The Impact on Society

Diversity and representation in pop culture have significant ramifications for society at large. They shape how individuals perceive themselves and others, influence cultural norms, and can drive social change. When pop culture reflects a broad spectrum of identities and experiences, it helps to validate the lives of those who may have previously felt marginalized. This validation can foster a sense of belonging, reduce feelings of isolation, and even impact mental health positively.

One of the most immediate and visible impacts of diverse representation is the increase in role models for various communities. For teenagers especially, seeing someone who looks like them or shares similar experiences in the media can be incredibly empowering. It invites them to dream bigger, achieve more, and believe that their identity won't be a barrier to success. These role models can also challenge stereotypes and broaden understanding among diverse groups.

Moreover, the broadening of representation promotes cultural exchange and understanding. When people are exposed to stories and characters from different backgrounds, it can reduce prejudices and foster empathy. It encourages viewers to see the world through different lenses, thereby gradually shifting societal attitudes toward greater inclusivity and acceptance. In today's increasingly globalized world, this cultural exchange is not just beneficial but essential for a cohesive society.

Yet, representation does not come without its challenges. Tokenism, where marginalized groups are included superficially to present an appearance of diversity, can be counterproductive. It's crucial that representation is authentic and layered, reflecting the complexities of identities rather than relying on stereotypes. When executed poorly, it can reinforce harmful narratives rather than dismantle them.

Positive representation also has an economic impact. Diverse stories and characters can attract a broader audience, leading to increased viewership and consumer loyalty. Brands and media companies that prioritize inclusion often find that their content resonates more deeply and widely. This isn't just about doing what's right; it's about smart business in a multicultural world. Companies like Netflix and Disney have increasingly embraced this strategy, often seeing significant returns on their investments in diverse content.

The ripple effects of diverse representation in pop culture extend into other areas of society. For instance, when mainstream media includes diverse characters and stories, it can influence other sectors such as advertising, fashion, and even politics. It signals to these industries that inclusivity is not just acceptable, but desirable. When political figures see the value in diversity popularized in media, they may be more likely to implement inclusive policies.

Educational settings also benefit from diverse representation in pop culture. Teachers and educators can use media examples to discuss broader social issues, facilitating conversations about race, gender, and identity in a way that's accessible to students. By integrating these discussions into the curriculum, educators can prepare students for a diverse world, promoting social harmony and understanding from a young age.

However, it's crucial to maintain a critical perspective. While progress has been made, there is still a long way to go. Many communities remain underrepresented or misrepresented, and efforts to address this must be ongoing and evolving. It's essential to keep pushing for genuine representation across all forms of media—not just in front of the camera but also behind it, influencing storytelling decisions at every level.

Social media continues to play a pivotal role in shaping and reflecting diversity. Platforms like Instagram, Twitter, and TikTok offer spaces where traditionally marginalized voices can share their stories and influence popular narratives. These platforms have democratized content creation, allowing those who might not have access to traditional platforms to gain visibility and impact. Social media influencers from diverse backgrounds can challenge mainstream portrayals and offer alternative narratives, contributing to a more comprehensive and multifaceted cultural landscape.

In many ways, the push for diversity and representation in pop culture mirrors broader societal movements for equality and justice. The struggles and triumphs we observe in the media often reflect the challenges and victories societies face in real life. This mirroring effect underscores the importance of continuing to advocate for inclusive representation. It's not just about numbers or visibility; it's about creating a world where everyone feels seen, heard, and valued.

At the heart of this phenomenon is the recognition that representation matters. It affects self-perception, social dynamics, and even the goals individuals set for themselves. When underrepresented groups see themselves portrayed positively and authentically, it can lead to profound shifts in societal structures and individual aspirations. The goal is to move towards a culture where diversity isn't just celebrated but is the norm, and where everyone has the chance to see themselves in the stories being told.

Ultimately, the growing diversity in pop culture offers hope for a more inclusive future. It suggests a world where our differences are not just acknowledged but embraced, a world where everyone's story has value and a place. For teenagers navigating their identities in this complex cultural landscape, this shift is more than just encouraging. It's inspiring. And it holds the promise of a brighter, more equitable future for all.

Chapter 9:
The Dark Side of Fame

Fame, with all its glitz and glamour, often paints a deceptively rosy picture, but peeling back the layers reveals a much harsher reality. For many influencers and pop culture icons, the relentless pressure of public life can lead to significant emotional and psychological challenges. Constant scrutiny, unrealistic expectations, and the never-ending demand to stay relevant can feel like a double-edged sword. While their lives are broadcast to adoring fans, the impact on their mental health is profound and often overlooked. Navigating this treacherous terrain requires resilience, support systems, and sometimes, stepping back to preserve one's well-being. In the end, the costs of fame remind us that behind every curated post and viral video, there's a human being grappling with the complexities that come with their digital persona.

The Pressure of Public Life

Living under constant public scrutiny can be both exhilarating and exhausting. For influencers and celebrities, the steady gaze of the public eye adds a layer of pressure that most people rarely experience. When every action, word, or even a casual expression can be instantly shared and scrutinized by millions, the stakes are incredibly high. This pressure can make even the smallest of mistakes feel like colossal failures.

For many influencers, managing their public persona becomes a full-time job. They have to constantly think about how to present themselves in a way that resonates with their audience while also protecting their own mental health and privacy. Balancing authenticity with the curated image they portray can be a significant source of stress. Imagine not being able to share a tough day or a personal failure without fearing a backlash or, worse, losing followers.

The rise of social media has only amplified this phenomenon. Platforms like Instagram, TikTok, and Twitter thrive on a continuous cycle of content creation and consumption. This environment creates an expectation for influencers to be always on—always creating, sharing, and engaging. The underlying fear of irrelevance or being 'canceled' can be overwhelming. Even taking a simple break from posting can lead to anxiety about losing touch with their audience and the brands that sponsor them.

Moreover, there's a significant emotional toll that comes from the constant need to maintain a perfect image online. Influencers often feel compelled to filter out any aspect of their lives that might be perceived negatively. This can lead to a disconnect between their online persona and their real selves. Over time, this can cause stress, anxiety, and even identity crises, as they struggle to discern where their real identity ends and their public persona begins.

The pressure of public life isn't just about maintaining an image; it's also about dealing with criticism and hate. Influencers are often subject to harsh and relentless scrutiny from the public. Every tweet, photo, or video is open to comments, and not all of them are going to be positive. It's a space that can breed negativity, with anonymous users feeling free to voice harsh criticism or hateful comments. Coping with this constant stream of feedback requires thick skin, as even constructive criticism can sometimes feel like a personal attack.

Then there are the fans, whose love and devotion can become a double-edged sword. While positive support can be uplifting and motivational, it can also lead to unrealistic expectations. Fans might expect influencers to remain static, preserving the version of themselves that led to their initial following. Any deviation from this image can lead to disappointment or even outrage among followers. This makes personal growth and change a delicate endeavor for influencers, as they have to tread carefully between evolving as individuals and maintaining their brand.

Family and friends of influencers aren't immune to this pressure either. Their private lives can inadvertently become public fodder, leading to strained relationships and an added layer of stress. The invasion of privacy extends beyond the influencer, enveloping those close to them. A casual family outing or a private celebration might suddenly be cast into the public eye, disrupting what could have been a normal life for their loved ones.

In some cases, younger influencers face even more intense pressure. Navigating fame during formative years can complicate their development. They're expected to act as role models, regardless of their age or personal readiness for this responsibility. This can stifle their ability to make mistakes and learn from them privately, as every misstep becomes a public spectacle.

Despite all these challenges, some influencers manage to find ways to cope with the pressure by establishing boundaries. Setting clear limits on what aspects of their lives they're willing to share can mitigate some of the stress. Others turn to support systems, like friends, family, or mental health professionals, to help them navigate the highs and lows of public life.

Collaboration among influencers can also create a sense of community and mutual support. With shared experiences, they can offer each other advice, encouragement, and solidarity. By recognizing the shared nature of their struggles, they can collectively advocate for mental health awareness and more realistic standards in the digital space.

Certain platforms are also stepping up to address these issues. Features like comment moderation, privacy settings, and mental health resources are becoming more common. These tools can help influencers create a safer, more supportive online environment for themselves and their followers.

Ultimately, the pressure of public life is an inescapable aspect of modern fame. It's a double-edged sword that brings both opportunities and challenges. Influencers and celebrities must navigate this landscape carefully, prioritizing their well-being while meeting the demands of their audience. The path to maintaining a healthy balance is unique for each individual, but the growing awareness of these pressures marks a positive step toward a more sustainable approach to fame.

As you navigate your own digital spaces and interactions with influencers, it's essential to remember the person behind the screen. They, too, are navigating the complexities of their public and private lives, seeking understanding and compassion from their audience. By fostering a more empathetic and supportive online community, we can help alleviate some of the pressures faced by those in the public eye.

Addressing Mental Health

Amid the glitz and glamour of fame, mental health often takes a substantial hit. It's not just the pressure of public life; it's a complex intersection of stress, anxiety, and often, a sense of isolation. For teenagers dreaming of influencer stardom, it's essential to understand these undercurrents. Because let's be honest, the reality behind the filtered photos and viral videos can be starkly different from what it appears on screen.

Consider the sheer pressure of maintaining a public persona. Imagine being under a perpetual spotlight where every move, every word, every outfit is scrutinized. Celebrities often talk about the feeling of living in a fishbowl, and for influencers, this concept is amplified by the immediacy and reach of social media. Constantly producing content that resonates with an audience is not just tiring; it's exhausting. This pressure often contributes to extreme stress and anxiety issues. When every post is a performance, the line between the online persona and the real person blurs, leading to identity crises and mental fatigue.

For many influencers, their rise to fame is often swift but unpredictable, leaving little room for mental preparation. The sudden change from relative anonymity to public figure can be jarring. This transition often disrupts normal routines and relationships, making it challenging to find a sense of normalcy. In a world where everyone is watching, mistakes aren't just personal—they're public spectacles. Even a minor slip-up can spark a wildfire of criticism, further anchoring feelings of anxiety and self-doubt. Because, let's face it, nobody can be perfect all the time.

Adding to this, there's the pervasive issue of cyberbullying. Negative comments, trolls, and hate messages can be relentless. No matter how thick-skinned one appears, incessant online harassment can erode self-esteem over time. For those who are still developing their sense of self, as many young influencers are, this can be particularly damaging. They find themselves caught between the desire to engage with their audience and the dread of facing the next wave of negativity.

Another significant factor is the echo chamber effect of social media platforms. Influencers often feel compelled to stay within the confines of what's popular or risk losing their audience. This can create an inescapable loop where they suppress their true thoughts and feelings to conform to expectations. The result? A growing sense of alienation from one's own identity, leading to increased feelings of loneliness and depression. Even in a space teeming with followers, the sense of true connection can be elusive.

Monetary aspects complicate matters further. Financial instability, despite apparent success, looms large. Many influencers rely on brand deals and sponsorships, which are often volatile and short-lived. The pressure to continually perform and stay relevant to secure these deals is immense. It's akin to freelancing with the added stress of visibility and competition. The uncertainty associated with this environment can aggravate existing mental health issues, creating a vicious cycle that's hard to break.

So, what can be done? Addressing mental health in the realm of fame requires a multi-faceted approach. Firstly, setting boundaries is crucial. Influencers need to learn the art of stepping back from their screens to find balance and recharge. Just like anyone else, they deserve time off without the guilt of "not engaging." Understanding that the world won't collapse if they take a break is liberating and necessary for long-term sustainability in their careers.

Secondly, seeking professional help should be normalized and encouraged. Therapy and counseling can offer a sanctuary where they can freely express concerns and anxieties without fear of judgment. Many influencers advocate for mental health awareness, yet fear the stigma of admitting their struggles. This paradox needs addressing; influencers should be encouraged to practice what they preach, making mental health support a routine part of their lives.

It's also essential to foster authentic connections. Surrounding themselves with people who value them for who they are, beyond their online personas, can provide a solid support network. This connection with the offline world is grounding and can help in maintaining a healthy perspective on their fame and popularity. Encouraging influencers to participate in activities and communities away from the digital space can significantly enhance their mental well-being.

Additionally, building resilience is key. Influencers can benefit from training in handling criticism, understanding the nature of online harassment, and developing coping strategies. This resilience isn't about becoming immune to negative comments but rather about not letting those comments define their self-worth. Workshops and programs focusing on mental toughness and emotional intelligence could be incredibly beneficial.

Education around social media's impact on mental health should be a staple for budding influencers. This includes understanding how algorithms work, the reality behind virality, and the potential psychological pitfalls of fame. Awareness itself can be a powerful tool in combating the adverse effects of online life. At the end of the day, knowledge is power.

For those watching from the sidelines, it's crucial to remember that influencers are human, too. Empathy and kindness should be the baseline when engaging with them online. Promoting a culture of positivity can make a significant difference in mitigating the impact of cyberbullying and negativity. Collectively, we can shift the narrative from tearing down to building up.

The dark side of fame doesn't have to overshadow the potential for positive influence. By prioritizing mental health, influencers can not only enhance their well-being but also become healthier role models for their followers. It's a journey of self-discovery and resilience, one that redefines success not by the number of likes or followers but by personal happiness and fulfillment.

In conclusion, addressing mental health in the context of fame is indispensable. It's about creating a sustainable environment where influencers can thrive without compromising their mental well-being. This means setting realistic boundaries, seeking professional help, fostering authentic connections, building resilience, and educating themselves about the nuances of the digital world. Influencers, and by extension, their audience, stand to benefit immensely from a balanced approach to fame. After all, the ultimate goal is to live a fulfilling, self-compassionate, and mentally healthy life, whether one is in front of the camera or behind it.

Chapter 10:
Activism and Social Change

In today's digital age, influencers are not just content creators or trendsetters—they're also powerful catalysts for activism and social change. From climate change to social justice movements, these modern-day change-makers harness their vast platforms to amplify important issues and mobilize their followers into action. The immediacy and reach of social media mean that a single post can spark widespread awareness and participation, making every like, share, and comment a potential springboard for real-world impact. This dynamic environment encourages teenagers to see their own potential in contributing to positive change, using the tools and communities they interact with daily to advocate for the causes they care about. Whether it's promoting sustainability or supporting marginalized voices, influencers show that youth activism can thrive in the digital realm, transforming everyday online interactions into powerful movements for a better world.

Influencers as Activists

In recent years, influencers have moved far beyond just promoting the latest fashion trends or beauty products. They've realized the incredible power they wield and have begun using their platforms to advocate for social change. This growing trend of influencers as activists is reshaping how young people engage with important issues and prompting significant shifts in societal attitudes.

When prominent influencers speak out on social issues, their vast audiences take notice. Historically, social change relied heavily on traditional forms of media to spread awareness. Now, a single post on Instagram or TikTok can reach millions within hours. Influencers can spotlight issues ranging from climate change to racial injustice, amplifying voices that might otherwise go unheard. Their efforts are increasingly crucial in a digital world where attention spans are short, but the reach is vast.

A key factor driving this shift is authenticity. Followers trust influencers who present authentic, relatable content. They look to these figures not just for entertainment or lifestyle inspiration, but for guidance on societal issues. When influencers share their thoughts on activist causes, it feels personal and genuine, making their messages more impactful. Because of this trust, influencers can effectively mobilize their followers to take action, whether it's signing a petition, attending a protest, or donating to a cause.

Consider the role influencers played during the global Black Lives Matter movement. Many influencers used their platforms to share educational content, promote Black-owned businesses, and encourage their followers to support the cause. They posted stories, shared resources, and even participated in organized events. Their digital activism contributed significantly to the visibility and momentum of the movement.

One of the most powerful aspects of influencer activism is the ability to make activism accessible. Young people, who might otherwise feel disconnected from traditional forms of protest or advocacy, can engage with these issues in a familiar and approachable digital space. This accessibility breaks down barriers and makes it easier for people to get involved, fostering a new generation of socially conscious individuals.

Moreover, influencers often collaborate with each other to further amplify their messages. These collaborations can range from joint campaigns to combined charity efforts, leveraging the power of multiple platforms for a greater reach. By uniting their voices, influencers can create powerful waves of change and draw attention to critical issues that need urgent action.

However, the role of influencers as activists is not without its challenges. There is a fine line between genuine activism and performative actions. Performative activism occurs when influencers engage in social issues for clout or to appease their audience without a real commitment to the cause. This can be detrimental, as it may lead to cynicism and skepticism among followers. Thus, it is crucial for influencers to engage sincerely and consistently with the issues they advocate, maintaining transparency about their motivations and actions.

Another challenge is the backlash that influencers might face when they take a stand. Addressing socially or politically charged issues can be polarizing, resulting in loss of followers or negative comments. Despite the potential for backlash, many influencers continue to speak out, driven by the belief that their platform should be used for good. They understand that the impact of their activism can inspire others, fostering a culture of awareness and empathy.

In the realm of environmental activism, influencers like Greta Thunberg have shown how powerful youth voices can be in driving change. Although not a traditional social media influencer, her journey exemplifies how young people can harness online platforms to lead global movements. Many influencers draw inspiration from figures like Greta, using their own reach to advocate for sustainable practices and environmental policies.

Importantly, the impact of influencer activism extends beyond digital spaces. Influencers often encourage their followers to participate in real-world actions, blending online advocacy with offline efforts. This can include arranging meet-ups for clean-up drives, organizing fundraisers, or participating in marches and rallies. By providing tangible ways to get involved, influencers help bridge the gap between awareness and action.

The rise of influencers as activists also aligns with the broader trend of brands becoming more socially responsible. Influencers can put pressure on brands to adopt more ethical practices and support social causes. Many influencers now choose to work only with brands that align with their values, pushing the industry towards greater accountability and transparency. This symbiotic relationship benefits both influencers and the causes they champion, creating a ripple effect across various sectors.

Ultimately, the role of influencers as activists demonstrates the evolving nature of digital influence. It highlights the potential for significant, positive change driven by the leaders of online communities. Young people looking to engage with social issues can find role models in these influencers, who show that activism doesn't have to be confined to traditional methods. With a phone and a passion for justice, anyone can contribute to the movements shaping our world today.

As the landscape of influence continues to evolve, the intersection of social media and activism will likely become even more pronounced. Future influencers will build upon the foundation laid by today's digital activists, inspiring new generations to use their voices for good. This ongoing evolution not only democratizes activism but also ensures that critical social issues remain at the forefront of public discourse.

By understanding how influencers are leveraging their platforms for activism, digitally-savvy teens can better appreciate the power they hold in their virtual hands. They can learn to critically engage with the content they consume and be inspired to make their own mark on the world. The next wave of social change makers may well be the ones scrolling through their feeds today, ready to transform passion into action.

Digital Movements

In today's digital landscape, social movements are no longer confined to marches on the streets or sit-ins at significant locations. Instead, they have found a vibrant and efficacious home online, sparking change in ways that were unimaginable just a few decades ago. Digital movements harness the expansive reach of the internet, enabling activists to mobilize swiftly, gather support from all corners of the globe, and challenge injustices with greater immediacy.

One of the most powerful aspects of digital movements is their ability to amplify marginalized voices. Websites, social media platforms, and blogging sites have democratized the space for activism, allowing anyone with an internet connection to speak up and be heard. This phenomenon was prominently showcased by the #MeToo movement, where survivors of sexual harassment and assault shared their stories en masse, creating a ripple effect that resonated across industries and continents. The hashtag encapsulated a collective outcry that was impossible to ignore.

Similarly, the Black Lives Matter (BLM) movement, which started as a hashtag on social media, grew into a global campaign against systemic racism and violence toward Black individuals. The viral spread of videos documenting police brutality highlighted issues that mainstream media often overlooked. With platforms like Twitter, Instagram, and TikTok, activists could educate the public, share resources, and organize protests in real-time. The hashtag #BlackLivesMatter became a rallying cry, uniting people worldwide in the fight for justice and equality.

These digital movements have a few key features in common. Firstly, they rely heavily on visual content—images and videos—that can elicit strong emotional responses and prompt action. A photo of a peaceful protest or a video capturing an instance of injustice can go viral within hours, sparking outrage and mobilization. This visual element makes the issues at hand tangible and urgent, compelling viewers to engage and react.

Another critical feature is the use of storytelling. Personal narratives humanize the causes and make them relatable. When activists share their stories, they bridge the gap between the movement and the everyday experiences of their audience. This approach fosters empathy and solidarity, driving home the importance of the cause. Social media platforms have built-in tools—like Instagram Stories, Facebook Live, and Twitter threads—that facilitate this kind of engagement.

Pivotal to the success of digital movements is the role of influencers. With their substantial followings and strong engagement rates, influencers have the power to bring attention to social issues and mobilize their audiences. Some influencers dedicate their platforms to activism, while others incorporate social issues into their content. For instance, after the horrific mass shooting at Marjory Stoneman Douglas High School, students like Emma González became influential voices in the gun control debate. Their social media presence helped maintain the momentum of the conversation, making it a persistent topic in public discourse.

The inherent flexibility of digital platforms also means that these movements can adapt quickly to changing circumstances. During the COVID-19 pandemic, for example, physical protests and gatherings were restricted. Yet, activists found new ways to advocate for their causes. Online petitions, virtual town halls, and informational webinars became popular methods for maintaining activism. Digital campaigns such as #CancelRent or #ProtectEssentialWorkers emerged to address the specific challenges posed by the pandemic, demonstrating the resiliency and adaptability of digital movements.

In this ever-connected digital age, one significant benefit is the ability to crowdsource information and resources. This aspect was vividly demonstrated during the early days of the COVID-19 pandemic, when reliable information was in high demand and often hard to come by. Grassroots movements like the Mutual Aid networks stepped in to fill the gaps, using social media to coordinate and distribute resources like food, medical supplies, and financial assistance to those in need. These initiatives allowed communities to self-organize effectively, leveraging the power of digital connectivity to provide immediate relief and support.

Global reach and inclusivity are essential components that set digital movements apart from traditional forms of activism. Movements no longer need to rely on national borders or physical proximity to gain traction. Activists from different cultural backgrounds and geographical locations can collaborate seamlessly, creating a more inclusive and diversified approach to social change. For example, climate activism has seen a surge in international collaboration, with activists from various countries uniting under the common goal of addressing climate change. The Fridays for Future movement, initiated by Swedish activist Greta Thunberg, underscores the global nature of digital activism, inspiring students worldwide to strike for climate action.

Of course, digital movements are not without their challenges. Online activism can sometimes fall into the trap of "slacktivism," where individuals express support for a cause without committing to any tangible action. Sharing a hashtag is easy, but real change requires sustained effort and participation beyond the screen. Additionally, the fast-paced and often fleeting nature of social media can mean that important issues quickly fade from public attention. Effective movements must find ways to maintain momentum and translate digital support into real-world outcomes.

There's also the issue of misinformation and the spread of false narratives, which can undermine the legitimacy of digital movements. Activists must navigate the complex landscape of truth and deception, often facing coordinated efforts to discredit their causes. Fact-checking and media literacy have become essential tools in the digital activist's arsenal. Platforms are increasingly implementing measures to combat fake news, but the responsibility also lies with users to verify information and critically evaluate the sources they encounter.

Moreover, the algorithms that govern social media platforms can either amplify or hinder digital movements. While algorithms can help content go viral, they can also create echo chambers or suppress visibility. Activists and influencers need to understand how these algorithms work to optimize their reach and impact. The strategic use of hashtags, timing of posts, and engagement with followers all play a role in navigating the digital landscape effectively.

As the digital world continues to evolve, so too will the strategies and tools used by activists. Emerging technologies like artificial intelligence, virtual reality, and blockchain hold potential for new forms of activism. Virtual reality can provide immersive experiences that foster empathy and understanding, while blockchain can offer decentralized platforms for organizing and funding movements. These technologies could revolutionize the way activists engage with their audiences and create lasting change.

In conclusion, digital movements have transformed the landscape of activism, making it more accessible, immediate, and far-reaching. They empower individuals to speak out, collaborate, and effect change on a global scale. However, successful digital activism requires more than just a viral hashtag—it's about sustained effort, adaptability, and a deep understanding of the digital tools at one's disposal. For the digitally-savvy teenager, the potential to be a catalyst for social change has never been greater. By harnessing the power of digital platforms, they can contribute to movements that resonate across borders and impact lives. The future of activism is undeniably digital, and the next wave of changemakers is already here, ready to lead the charge.

Chapter 11:
Fan Culture and Community Building

F an culture has always been more than just admiration—it's about creating a sense of belonging. In today's digital world, this extends to communities where fans interact, share content, and engage in conversations that amplify their passion. These communities, often centered around influencers and their digital presence, become unique ecosystems fueled by shared interests and collective activities. Active participation, whether through comments, fan art, or related discussions, builds lasting connections and fosters a supportive environment. This engagement not only strengthens the bond between influencers and their audiences but also cultivates a space for fans to express themselves and find camaraderie. It's here that the line between creator and audience blurs, creating an interactive and dynamic reality where every "like," "share," and response contributes to a thriving community.

The Role of Fan Communities

Fan communities are at the heart of pop culture and community building, serving as vibrant ecosystems where fans connect over shared passions. These communities provide a sense of belonging, fostering relationships that often transcend digital spaces to influence our real-world interactions. Whether it's through Reddit threads, Discord servers, or even in-person meetups, fan communities are dynamic spaces that offer a third place—a social environment separate from home and work—where fans can feel understood and valued.

One of the most compelling aspects of fan communities is how they democratize influence. Outside the mainstream avenues of media and celebrity channels, fan communities create a space where anyone with a shared enthusiasm can contribute, grow, and influence others. In these settings, it's not just about passively consuming content but actively shaping the narrative through discussions, fan art, and even fan fiction. This participatory culture fosters creativity and can even propell individuals within the community to become micro-influencers in their own right.

What make fan communities particularly unique are their inclusive ecosystems. They serve as melting pots where diverse voices and perspectives are celebrated. Within these spaces, it is not unusual to find individuals from various backgrounds and lifestyles converging to discuss common interests. This diversity enriches the discussions and often leads to a more profound understanding of the content being celebrated. Furthermore, the global reach of social media has made it possible for fans from different parts of the world to engage with each other, breaking down geographical barriers and making the world feel a little bit smaller.

Fan communities also play a crucial role in ensuring the longevity of a cultural phenomenon. Pop culture trends can be fleeting, but the communities built around them often endure long after the spotlight has faded. For instance, consider the enduring appeal of cult classics or TV shows that have long ended but still command a dedicated fanbase. These communities often engage in activities like rewatching episodes, hosting fan conventions, and even advocating for revivals, thereby making an indelible mark on the cultural landscape.

It's worth considering how these communities impact the influencers themselves. For online personalities, the feedback loop created by fan communities can be both uplifting and constructive. Positive reinforcement from a dedicated fanbase can serve as a motivational tool, encouraging influencers to continue producing content. On the flip side, constructive criticism offered within a supportive community can help influencers refine their craft and evolve in ways that resonate more deeply with their audience.

Moreover, fan communities provide a fertile ground for networking and collaboration. For emerging influencers or artists, these networks offer invaluable opportunities to connect with like-minded individuals, share resources, and even initiate collaborations that might not have been possible otherwise. This collaborative spirit not only helps in personal growth but also propels the entire community forward, making it a hub for innovation and new ideas.

However, the influence of fan communities isn't confined to the digital realm alone. Many of these groups take their enthusiasm offline through fan conventions, meetups, and other events. These physical gatherings strengthen the bonds formed online and allow for more intimate and personal interactions. Such events often become landmark experiences for fans, creating memories and friendships that last a lifetime. They also offer influencers an opportunity to engage with their audience in a more tangible, impactful manner.

Beyond personal connections, fan communities have shown their power to drive social change. Organized groups of devoted fans can mobilize to support causes that align with the values of their favorite influencers or content. Many fan communities have spearheaded fundraising campaigns, petition drives, and awareness efforts that have had real-world impacts. By channeling their collective passion, they can make a substantial difference on issues ranging from social justice to environmental conservation.

In essence, fan communities are more than just clusters of admiration. They are living, breathing entities that evolve with the cultural phenomena they support. They create spaces of learning, acceptance, and creativity, contributing to personal growth and collective empowerment. For teenagers navigating the complexities of identity and belonging, these communities offer a supportive network where they can explore their interests freely and connect with others who share their passions.

Ultimately, the role of fan communities in pop culture and community building is multifaceted. They are not just passive recipients of content but active participants in a dynamic and symbiotic relationship with influencers and the content they cherish. Whether through initiating trends, providing emotional support, or driving societal change, fan communities are vital pillars in the landscape of modern pop culture.

Engagement and Interaction

In the vibrant world of pop culture, the relationship between influencers and their fans is deeply symbiotic. This bond thrives on active engagement and interaction. Fans are no longer just passive consumers; they're integral to the content creation cycle, often shaping the direction of their favorite influencers' careers. To understand the depth of this engagement, let's delve into the mechanics that make it possible.

One of the most significant ways influencers engage with their fans is through social media platforms. These platforms offer direct lines of communication, allowing influencers to touch the lives of their followers in real-time. Whether it's through a live-streaming session on Instagram or a Q&A on TikTok, the power of instant connection cannot be overstated. Fans feel seen and heard, fostering a sense of community that's both personal and expansive.

Imagine your favorite YouTuber shouting you out during a live stream or responding to your comment on their latest video. This kind of direct interaction makes fans feel valued, enhancing their loyalty and fortifying the influencer's brand. Genuine engagement consistently turns followers into fervent advocates, driving a cycle of organic growth that's hard to replicate through any other means.

Moreover, the rise of interactive features on social media platforms has enabled influencers to create content that's engaging and participatory. Polls, quizzes, and challenges are more than mere gimmicks; they invite fans to be part of the narrative. When an influencer asks their followers for opinions on potential content ideas or invites them to partake in a trending challenge, it makes followers feel like valuable contributors.

Community forums and private groups are other crucial components in building and maintaining engagement. Platforms like Discord, Reddit, and Facebook groups provide dedicated spaces for fans to discuss, critique, and celebrate their favorite content. These forums often become incubators for deeper engagement, where sub-communities flourish around niche interests within the broader fanbase.

It's essential to recognize the role of collaboration in this ecosystem. Joint projects, guest appearances, and collaborative content between influencers and their peers often invigorate fan communities. Cross-promotion not only broadens reach but adds layers of interaction, bringing together fragmented audiences and fostering collective enthusiasm.

Looking at the phenomenon of "fan art" and "fan fiction," one can see how fan engagement extends beyond passive consumption. By producing their own creative works based on their favorite influencers or pop culture icons, fans add value to the community. Influencers who acknowledge and celebrate these fan-made contributions often see heightened levels of loyalty and interaction. User-generated content becomes a pivotal part of the community's narrative, reinforcing a shared culture and identity.

Moreover, modern fans expect transparency and authenticity from their influencers. Gone are the days when a perfectly curated feed was enough to maintain engagement. Today's digitally-savvy teenagers value authenticity over perfection. When influencers openly discuss their struggles, share behind-the-scenes content, or simply talk about their daily lives, they build trust. This transparency not only humanizes influencers but makes their followers feel closer to them, further blurring the lines between virtual and real-life connections.

Alongside transparency, relatability plays a crucial role. Influencers who can strike a chord with their audience's daily experiences—be it through humor, shared struggles, or common interests—find it easier to maintain sustained engagement. Relatable content that reflects the lives and aspirations of the audience forms a sturdy foundation for deeper interaction.

Controversy, while often seen as negative, can also precipitate higher levels of engagement. When managed correctly, addressing controversies can provide a platform for meaningful dialogue. Influencers who navigate these turbulent waters with grace and candor often emerge stronger, with a more engaged and supportive fanbase.

The importance of feedback can't be overlooked in the cycle of engagement. Active listening is key. Influencers who take the time to read and act on their followers' suggestions, complaints, and compliments indicate that they value their community. Implementing popular fan suggestions or addressing critical feedback transparently closes the loop of communication, reinforcing a sense of community ownership.

Influencers occasionally meet their fans face-to-face through meet-and-greet events, fan conventions, and pop-up appearances. These offline interactions add a layer of intimacy and reality to the digital engagement, forming memories that followers cherish for a lifetime. Such events can transform casual followers into lifelong fans, elevating the influencer's cultural clout both online and offline.

Live interactions don't just happen in real life; they are also a digital affair. Live streaming events have brought new dimensions to fan engagement. Platforms like Twitch and YouTube allow influencers to engage with fans in real-time, creating dynamic conversations and spontaneous moments that deeply resonate with audiences. Even those unable to join the livestream often watch the recorded sessions later, maintaining a sense of connection.

During these live sessions, influencers often engage in playful banter, answer burning questions, and share exclusive content. The immediacy of live interaction adds excitement and unpredictability, creating a sense of a shared experience that strengthens the community bond. Feeling part of an interactive experience makes fans feel special, cementing their loyalty and boosting engagement.

It's not just about what influencers say but also how they say it. Thoughtful communication that acknowledges fans' contributions and celebrates their uniqueness often sets successful influencers apart. Personalized interactions, be it through direct messages, comments, or shout-outs, leave lasting impressions that foster intense loyalty and engagement.

In conclusion, the landscape of fan engagement and interaction is multifaceted, driven by direct communication, collaborative ventures, and genuine transparency. In a world that's increasingly digital, these elements create communities that are not only bound by a shared interest in pop culture but are also dynamic, engaged, and ever-evolving. Influencers who master the art of engagement transform their followings from mere audiences to active, vibrant communities. This transformation is at the heart of the profoundly impactful relationship between influencers and their fans in modern pop culture.

Chapter 12:
The Future of Influencing

Looking ahead, the landscape of influencing is bound to become even more dynamic and immersive. With advancements in augmented reality (AR) and virtual reality (VR), influencers will craft experiences that are not just seen, but felt. Artificial intelligence (AI) will likely play a significant role in personalizing content to unprecedented levels, making interactions more meaningful and targeted. As new social platforms emerge, they will redefine how influencers connect with their audiences, pushing the boundaries of creativity and engagement. The future will also bring more emphasis on authenticity and social responsibility, as followers demand transparency and positive impact from those they support. Teens, poised to be the driving force behind these shifts, will not only consume content but also shape the trends and values of tomorrow's digital ecosystem.

Emerging Trends

As we peer into the crystal ball of the influencer world, it's clear that massive transformations are underway. The landscape is rich with innovation, shifting dynamics, and technological advancements that promise to redefine the very essence of influence. These emerging trends aren't just shaping influencers' lives but also the way we, as a society, engage with content and popular culture.

One of the most noticeable trends is the rise of micro and nano influencers. While the big names still rule the roost, there's a growing preference for influencers with smaller, more niche followings. These influencers tend to have more engaged followers and can deliver content that feels genuine and relatable. Brands are increasingly recognizing the value of authenticity over sheer numbers, making these smaller influencers invaluable. They connect on a personal level, crafting content that's often more relevant to their communities.

Moreover, virtual influencers are stepping into the spotlight. These digitally-created personalities, like Lil Miquela and Shudu, captivate millions without actually existing in the physical world. The allure lies in their perfect blend of reality and fantasy, offering a futuristic take on identity and presence. As technology continues to advance, we can expect more sophisticated and interactive virtual influencers that challenge our perception of authenticity.

Interactive content is another trend that's gaining momentum. Live streams and real-time interaction have become critical tools for engagement. The audience craves connection, and influencers are leveraging this by creating content that allows followers to interact instantly. Whether it's through live Q&As, real-time challenges, or interactive polls, the relationship between influencers and their audience continues to deepen.

Another significant development is the integration of augmented reality (AR) and virtual reality (VR) into influencer content. These technologies offer immersive experiences that go beyond traditional media. Imagine trying on virtual outfits recommended by fashion influencers or attending exclusive VR concerts hosted by your favorite musicians. This shift is not just innovative but also opens up new dimensions of engagement, providing followers with experiences they couldn't have dreamed of before.

As we move forward, the line between influencer and entrepreneur is blurring. Influencers are no longer just content creators; they are becoming brand owners, launching their products, and diversifying their income streams. The rise of influencer-led brands—from makeup lines to clothing collections—demonstrates the tremendous impact an influencer can have on the market. This trend is empowering creators, allowing them to maintain creative control while building substantial business empires.

The importance of data and analytics cannot be overstated. Influencers and brands are now armed with sophisticated tools to measure engagement, track trends, and understand their audience's preferences in real-time. This data-driven approach not only enhances the quality of the content but also ensures that it resonates with the targeted audience. By leveraging analytics, influencers can tailor their strategies to maximize impact and effectiveness.

In parallel, the focus on mental health and well-being is becoming more pronounced. The pressures of maintaining an online persona, coupled with constant scrutiny, are leading influencers and their followers to prioritize mental wellness. Influencers openly discussing their mental health struggles are fostering a more supportive online community. This trend highlights the need for a balanced approach to social media, advocating for self-care amidst the digital hustle.

Inclusivity and representation continue to be crucial themes in the influencer space. There's a growing demand for diverse voices and stories that reflect the audience's varied experiences. Influencers are using their platforms to champion social justice, challenge stereotypes, and promote inclusivity. This trend signifies a broader cultural shift towards accepting and celebrating differences, which has a profound impact on how communities are built online.

Sustainability is yet another emerging trend that's gaining traction. As awareness about environmental issues grows, both influencers and their audiences are becoming more eco-conscious. From promoting sustainable products to advocating for environmentally friendly practices, influencers play a pivotal role in driving the conversation around sustainability. This shift towards a more conscious way of living is changing consumer behaviors and encouraging brands to adopt greener practices.

The advent of new social media platforms is also worth noting. While giants like Instagram and TikTok continue to dominate, newer platforms are cropping up with unique features that cater to different audiences. These platforms offer alternative spaces for creativity and expression, offering influencers fresh opportunities to showcase their talents and connect with their followers in novel ways.

Looking ahead, the role of artificial intelligence in content creation will likely expand. AI-driven tools can assist influencers in various aspects of their work—from editing videos to generating captions and even personalizing content for individual followers. This integration can enhance productivity and creativity, allowing influencers to focus more on engaging with their audience and less on mundane tasks.

Lastly, blockchain technology holds promise for addressing some of the industry's long-standing issues, such as transparency and intellectual property rights. By leveraging blockchain, influencers can ensure that their content's provenance is secure, and that they receive fair compensation for their work. It also opens up possibilities for creating decentralized platforms that offer greater control and ownership to the creators themselves.

The future of influencing is teeming with exciting possibilities. While the landscape will undoubtedly continue to evolve, the core principles of authenticity, connection, and innovation remain steadfast. As we navigate this dynamic ecosystem, these emerging trends remind us of the endless creativity and potential that lies at the intersection of technology and human influence.

The Evolution of Digital Influence

Digital influence has seen a remarkable transformation over the years. Once, the idea of influencing others in the digital realm revolved around simple blog posts and emails. Today, it's a multifaceted landscape where social media platforms, algorithms, and user engagement coalesce to create powerful ripple effects. The arc of this evolution isn't just about technological advancements; it's about how individuals have harnessed these tools to redefine fame, influence, and relationship-building.

It all started with the humble beginnings of the internet. Forums and chat rooms allowed people to share ideas, opinions, and information. Fast forward to the early 2000s, and platforms like MySpace and Blogger enabled larger-scale personal expression. Although rudimentary by today's standards, these tools laid the groundwork for the profound digital influence we see now. These early platforms provided the building blocks for today's more sophisticated social networks.

Social media giants like Facebook, Twitter, and Instagram revolutionized digital influence in the late 2000s and early 2010s. These platforms introduced a new form of celebrity – the social media star – which offered a more democratic form of fame. Instead of studios, record labels, or publishers controlling who achieved fame, everyday individuals could now reach massive audiences. This shift was monumental, as it removed traditional gatekeepers and enabled more diverse voices to be heard. Suddenly, anyone with a smartphone could become an influencer.

The rise of multimedia content further propelled the dynamic of digital influence. With the advent of high-speed internet and smartphones, videos became integral to online presence. YouTube emerged as a significant platform, enabling content creators to build massive followings through vlogs, tutorials, and entertainment videos. The visual appeal and relatability of video content made it easier for influencers to connect with their audience on a deeper level. This connection was less about crafted personas and more about authenticity, or at least the semblance of it.

Algorithms played a crucial role in this evolution. On platforms like Instagram and TikTok, algorithms determine what content gets seen and what doesn't. This can turn an unknown creator into an overnight sensation by making their content go viral. Influencers have had to master these algorithms to maintain and grow their visibility. Understanding these ever-changing algorithms and leveraging them effectively became essential skills for anyone looking to wield digital influence.

Transparency and authenticity became key trends in digital influence. Audiences grew savvier and more discerning. They started valuing authenticity over polished, advertising-like content. Influencers who were honest, open, and genuine about their lives and struggles garnered more trust and loyalty from their followers. This trend turned influencers into role models who could lead by example, promote positive societal changes, and inspire their audiences in meaningful ways.

Social media platforms themselves have evolved in response to how influencers use them. Features like Instagram Stories, IGTV, Snapchat Discover, and Facebook Live were introduced to offer more content formats. These changes provided influencers with new ways to engage their audiences and expanded their content strategies. Each new feature or platform update demanded adaptability and creativity from influencers. It was no longer enough to be good at one type of content; versatility became essential.

Brands quickly caught on to the potential of digital influence, leading to a new economy. Sponsorships, brand collaborations, and ambassadorships emerged as lucrative business opportunities for influencers. These partnerships allowed brands to authentically reach their target audiences through trusted voices. The commercial aspect of influencing has grown so much that it's not uncommon for influencers to earn millions from brand deals, effectively turning digital influence into a legitimate career path.

As digital influence continues to evolve, we see the rise of niche communities and micro-influencers. Unlike mega-influencers with millions of followers, micro-influencers may have smaller, but highly engaged and loyal, follower bases. Their close-knit communities often result in higher engagement rates and more meaningful interactions. Brands have taken note of this trend, realizing that partnering with micro-influencers can yield higher ROI despite their smaller follower counts.

One of the fascinating aspects of digital influence is how it's continually shaped by emerging technologies. Virtual and augmented reality, for instance, are starting to blur the lines between the digital and the physical worlds. These technologies could revolutionize how influencers interact with their audiences, offering immersive experiences that were previously unimaginable. This signals a future where digital influence will be even more interactive and engaging.

Gen Z and their digital nativity have also played a significant role in this evolution. Growing up with the internet, this generation is incredibly adept at navigating digital spaces. They're not just passive consumers; they're active participants who create content, engage with influencers, and even become influencers themselves. Their preferences and behaviors will undoubtedly shape the future of digital influence, pushing it towards even more personalization, immediacy, and authenticity.

The path of digital influence is a testament to the innovative spirit of individuals and the adaptability of human nature. From its humble beginnings to the complex, flourishing ecosystem it is today, digital influence will continue to evolve, reflecting changes in technology and societal values. As we look towards the future, the only certainty is that the landscape of digital influence will keep shifting, driven by new platforms, new technologies, and new voices waiting to be heard.

Conclusion

A s we draw this exploration to a close, it's important to reflect on the vast landscape we've traversed. Pop culture and the influencers who dominate it have shaped our world in ways both visible and subtle. From the content we consume daily to the trends that define our generation, the influence of these digital tastemakers is both profound and pervasive.

The evolution of influence has demonstrated how ordinary individuals can rise to extraordinary prominence. Social media stars have become household names, their reach extending far beyond their initial platforms. This transformation was propelled by algorithms that amplify virality and the strategic efforts of influencers to build and maintain their online presence. The once-linear pathway to fame now branches in numerous, often unpredictable directions.

In the realm of music, we've seen how streaming services have revolutionized the industry. Influencers play a significant role in shaping musical tastes, often driving the success of new artists and tracks. Similarly, in the world of fashion, social media has given rise to new icons, who dictate trends to millions of followers. These influencers provide an instant, relatable source of style inspiration, further blurring the line between celebrity and everyday life.

Film and television have not been immune to this shift. The power of YouTube stars demonstrates how digital platforms can serve as springboards to mainstream success. Cross-platform popularity solidifies their presence, creating a new breed of celebrity who adeptly navigates multiple channels to reach their audience.

Social media platforms themselves are integral to this narrative. From the visual appeal of Instagram to the short-form creativity of TikTok, each platform offers unique opportunities for influencers to connect with their audience. Understanding these platforms is crucial for anyone looking to carve out a space in the digital world.

The economics of influence reveal how monetizing this new form of celebrity is both an art and a science. Sponsorships, brand collaborations, and other revenue streams enable influencers to turn their passion into profit. Yet, this financial aspect brings its own set of challenges and ethical considerations, requiring a delicate balance between authenticity and commercial interests.

Diversity and representation in pop culture are crucial for fostering an inclusive society. Influencers from various backgrounds bring fresh perspectives, challenging stereotypes and promoting a more equitable cultural landscape. This inclusion has a ripple effect, influencing societal norms and encouraging broader acceptance.

However, fame does have its dark side. The pressure of maintaining a public persona can take a toll on mental health, underscoring the need for supportive environments and open dialogues about well-being. Addressing these challenges is essential for sustainable success in the influencer sphere.

On a brighter note, influencers have also become powerful agents of social change. Digital movements and activism led by these figures demonstrate the potential for positive impact, leveraging their reach to advocate for important causes and mobilize communities.

Fan culture plays a pivotal role in this ecosystem. The communities built around influencers provide a sense of belonging and engagement that extends beyond mere content consumption. These interactions create a dynamic, interactive space where fans and influencers can grow together.

Looking to the future, the landscape of digital influence continues to evolve. Emerging trends and technologies will shape the next generation of influencers, driving innovation and new forms of connection. The digital era promises to remain vibrant and ever-changing, with endless possibilities for those willing to adapt and push boundaries.

Ultimately, the world of pop culture and influencers is a testament to the power of connection in the digital age. It's a realm where creativity, community, and commerce intersect, offering both challenges and opportunities. For the curious and digitally-savvy teenager, understanding this landscape is not just about recognizing trends, but about seeing the potential for their own impact and influence in this interconnected world.

As we close this journey, remember that you have the power to shape your own narrative. Use the insights gained to navigate the digital landscape wisely, to create and connect authentically, and to contribute positively to the ever-evolving realm of pop culture. Your voice matters, and your influence can make a difference.

Appendix A:
Appendix

This Appendix provides additional resources and insights to further enhance your understanding of the topics discussed throughout the book. While the chapters delve into the various facets of pop culture and influencer impact, this section serves as a supplementary guide to deepen your exploration and learning.

1. Recommended Readings

Here are some books, articles, and research papers that offer valuable perspectives on the subjects covered:

- **Understanding Media: The Extensions of Man** by Marshall McLuhan

- **Fans, Bloggers, and Gamers: Exploring Participatory Culture** by Henry Jenkins

- **It's Complicated: The Social Lives of Networked Teens** by Danah Boyd

- **The Influencer Economy: How to Launch Your Idea, Share It with the World, and Thrive in the Digital Age** by Ryan Williams

2. Key Influencer Platforms

To gain a practical understanding of how influencers operate, it's useful to become familiar with the platforms they use the most. Here's a brief overview:

- **Instagram:** Known for its visual content and micro-influencers.

- **YouTube:** A major hub for video content and a variety of niche communities.

- **TikTok:** The platform for viral trends and short-form entertainment.

- **Twitter:** Ideal for real-time interaction and following trending topics.

- **Snapchat:** Popular among younger demographics for its ephemeral content.

3. Influencer Toolkits

For those interested in becoming influencers or understanding the tools of the trade, consider these resources:

- **Analytics Tools:** These help measure the reach and engagement of posts. Popular options include Google Analytics, Hootsuite, and Sprout Social.

- **Content Creation Tools:** Tools like Canva for graphics, Adobe Premiere Pro for video editing, and Buffer for social media scheduling can be invaluable.

- **Monetization Tools:** Platforms like Patreon, Ko-fi, and various affiliate marketing programs can help monetize your influence.

4. Online Courses and Workshops

Numerous online educational platforms offer courses on digital marketing, social media strategies, and brand building. Some recommended platforms include:

- **Coursera:** Offers courses from leading universities and companies.

- **Udemy:** Provides practical courses from industry experts.

- **Skillshare:** Focuses on creative skills and community learning.

5. Key Organizations and Communities

Being part of influencer and pop culture communities can provide support and networking opportunities:

- **Influencer Marketing Hub:** A resource for influencer marketing news, tips, and tools.

- **Women in Influencer Marketing (WIIM):** A networking group that offers education and support.

- **Creator Insider:** YouTube's official channel for content creators.

This appendix is designed to be a springboard for further exploration and understanding. By utilizing these resources, you can deepen your insight into the dynamic world of pop culture and influencers, and maybe even carve out your own space in this exciting landscape.